FROM LOCKE TO MONTESSORI

A CRITICAL ACCOUNT OF THE MONTESSORI
POINT OF VIEW

BY

WILLIAM BOYD M.A. B.Sc. D.Phil.

Lecturer in Education in the University of Glasgow

LONDON

GEORGE G. HARRAP & COMPANY

2 & 3 PORTSMOUTH STREET KINGSWAY W.C.

1914

THE RIVERSIDE PRESS LIMITED, EDINBURGH

Introduction

that only those who believe in a particular educational doctrine can put it to the test of experiment. No doubt there is a circle in the argument when only those who believe in a system are recognized as qualified to prove its truth. But though such a circle would be vicious in the physical and the biological sciences (from which Dr Montessori derives her ' scientific method ') it is not merely permissible but inevitable in those branches of knowledge which take cognisance of the spiritual life of man and its manifestations in conduct. It is one of the postulates of ethics, for example, that only the good man can know what goodness means.[1] So in education, we never have methods of a purely objective order which produce their effects apart from the personal convictions of those who administer them. There may be special devices detachable from their context in a whole scheme which are of general application, but only those who teach in the spirit of a system are capable of adequately demonstrating its possibilities. Consequently the proof or disproof of the Montessori or any other method, so far as that depends on actual experience, must be left to those who believe in it. There is no argument for an educational method so conclusive as the permanent establishment of it in a working form.

[1] *Cf.* Aristotle, *Ethics*, Book I, ch. iv. The same idea is expressed in John vii. 17.

From Locke to Montessori

But that does not mean that we must await the success or the failure of the exponents of a particular conception of education in giving it practical shape before passing judgment on its merits. In the case of a scheme like that of Montessori, that would be an absurd requirement. It will not be till we see the effects of her methods in the after-career of her pupils, first in school and professional training and afterwards in the business of ordinary life, that we shall have the materials for forming a complete judgment with regard to the practical efficiency of these methods. In the meantime, we have to make up our minds about their present worth for education. How is this to be done ? A scientific pedagogy, following the experimental method, can certainly give us some guidance in determining whether the general character of the system is consistent with what is most surely known about the development of mind, and whether as a matter of fact the immediate results claimed for the methods are what they are represented to be. But after a *prima-facie* case for further inquiry has been made out by these means there remain unanswered certain fundamental questions which are outside the scope of science (in the narrow acceptation of the term), because they involve, not judgments of fact, but judgments of worth. Especially we must know whether we are in substantial agreement with the general view of life taken by Dr Montessori before

Introduction

subscribing to her educational principles. The meaning we attach to the process of education and the end to which we suppose it to be directed are bound up with our working philosophy; and if we take a different view of our relations to the world and our fellow-men from hers, there must be a corresponding difference in our conception of education. Dr Montessori, indeed, attempts to evade such considerations by disclaiming all preconceptions with regard to the nature and purpose of education. But it is vain for one who includes among her basic principles ideas of profound metaphysical significance like freedom and individuality to pretend to dispense with philosophy in the work of educational reform; and equally vain for those who would understand her system to follow her in ignoring her philosophy.

Any effective criticism of Montessori and her methods must therefore in the long run direct itself to her fundamental ideas. For this reason, there is much to be gained by making the first approach to her system indirectly through a study of its ancestry in the world of ideas. She herself constantly invites her readers to take this way of comprehending her educational views by her generously persistent acknowledgment of her obligations to Itard and Seguin, the two great doctors who anticipated her in the yoking together of medicine and pedagogy. If, however, we are to appreciate fully the significance of this obligation of hers, we must go further back in the history of education than she has gone. Itard and Seguin were not really pioneers in a new conception of educational endeavour, as she seems to imagine. They were simply developing in a special direction the great revolutionary ideas about education which were first suggested by John Locke toward the end of the seventeenth century and afterwards enunciated most clearly and convincingly by Jean Jacques Rousseau. She herself in following their lead was therefore recreating for our age some of the master thoughts of the recent past as she understood them herself, and so helping to carry forward a stage further the modern reconstruction of education.

PART I—HISTORICAL

CHAPTER I

JOHN LOCKE

1632–1704

JOHN LOCKE was brought up in a Puritan home in Somerset in the reign of Charles I, and was at Westminster School during the progress of the Civil War. He went up to the University of Oxford in the time of the Commonwealth, when Cromwell was Chancellor of the University, graduated Master of Arts, and lectured for some years on Greek, rhetoric, and moral philosophy. But though a successful student of the humanities, the bent of his mind was too practical for him to be long satisfied with the scholastic methods of the universities, and in 1666, at the age of thirty-four, he betook himself to experimental research in medicine. For a year or two he seems to have practised as a doctor in a private way, but, owing to a difference between the university authorities and himself, he only took the bachelor's degree in medicine and never completed his qualification. About this time he made the acquaintance of Lord Ashley (afterwards the first Earl of Shaftesbury), to whom he was attracted by their common love of liberty, and he entered his household as confidential secretary. Thus began a career, extending over many years, rich in intellectual and political interests, of which the chief literary outcome was the famous *Essay concerning Human Understanding*, published in 1690. Among the subjects to which his thoughts were turned during this period was the education of the young. When engaged in supervising the tuition of his master's son, and at a later time of his grandson, he gradually worked out the views which he published in 1693 as *Some Thoughts concerning Education*. This book, which is his only work dealing expressly with education, is not a systematic treatise on the subject. It was based on a series of informal letters written from Holland, to which he had gone when James II came to the throne, and it confined itself to the consideration of the upbringing of a gentleman's son under a tutor. His only other important work of an educational character was an essay entitled *Of the Conduct of the Understanding*, intended as a manual of self-instruction for young men, which was published after his death without his own revision.

Though both of these works were decidedly limited in their scope, they exercised a considerable influence on the current discussion of educational questions both in England and on the Continent.

John Locke

To some extent, no doubt, the attention paid to them was due to the great reputation of the *Essay concerning Human Understanding* rather than to their intrinsic merits. But with all their limitations they were worthy of the attention they got; for they had implicit in them a new conception of education which was destined to play almost as great and as varied a part in the development of educational doctrine as the new point of view of the *Essay* in the development of philosophy. The *Essay* made individual experience the central theme of philosophical thought. The *Thoughts concerning Education* treated the individual pupil as the main concern of the educator.

This individualism had its roots deep in the movement of revolt against authority which culminated in the Revolution of 1688. But over and above the general political influences one can distinguish in Locke a more personal strain of thought derived from his professional experiences. "No science," says Dugald Stewart, "could have been chosen, more happily calculated than medicine, to prepare such a mind as that of Locke for the prosecution of those speculations which have immortalized his name." This remark made primarily with reference to Locke's philosophy applies with even greater aptness to his educational principles. What distinguishes him from the very considerable number of educators in the seventeenth century who like himself were up in arms against the educational traditions of the Renaissance as represented by the grammar schools was the fresh view he obtained by looking at scholastic questions from the medical standpoint. All through his discussion of education he thinks of the pupils as a doctor thinks of his patients—as individual cases to be diagnosed separately and to be dealt with by the methods best suited for their special temper and conditions.

In his own case, it is true, the combination of physician and pedagogue remained external, because he proceeded with the work of education on the assumption that body and mind are quite distinct entities that call for separate treatment. This is evident in the opening sentence of the *Thoughts*: "A sound mind in a sound body is a short but full description of a happy state in this world." He advises the educator to pay proper attention to the clay cottage, as he calls the body, but his main concern is with the inmate and not the cottage. Following out this idea, he begins his letters about education with a lengthy discussion of the means to promote health, which he sums up concisely thus: "Plenty of open air, exercise and sleep: plain diet, no wine or strong drink, and very little or no physic: not too warm and strait clothing: especially the head and feet kept cold, and the feet often used to cold water and exposed to wet." Then, having said all he has got to say about the care of the body, he passes on to speak of the culture of the mind as though it were a quite new topic : " Due care being had to keep the body in strength and vigour, so that it may be able to obey and execute the orders of the mind, the next and principal business is to set the mind right." The complete separation of body and mind, of health and education, thus explicitly made, is maintained throughout the book. Locke is either the doctor thinking of the body or the teacher training mind and soul ; but doctor and teacher rarely by any chance come together on common ground.

Further, it never seems to have occurred to Locke that the training of the senses, which is an important feature of the discipline of the body, is a matter for the teacher at all. Neither in the *Thoughts concerning Education*, which refer to early life, nor in the short treatise on the *Conduct of the Understanding*, intended for students of more advanced years, is there the slightest indication that he was conscious of any need for such a training. This is the more surprising because his whole philosophy is based on the assumption that the mind of man depends for the materials with which it works on the impressions made by external objects on the senses. " Since there appear not to be any ideas in the mind before the senses have conveyed any in," he says in the *Essay*, " I conceive that ideas in the understanding

23

are coeval with sensation, which is such an impression or motion made in some part of the body as produces some perception in the understanding." [1] He is, indeed, aware that the senses get some kind of training at some point or other. When ' the learned and worthy Mr Molineux ' asks what would happen in the case of a man born blind who had received his sight after reaching manhood and suggests that the man would be quite unable to connect what he saw with what he already knew through touch, Locke expresses himself as in entire agreement, and adds that he leaves the question with his reader " as an occasion for him to consider how much he may be beholden to experience, improvement, and acquired notions." [2] Nevertheless he himself has no clear idea of the way in which the connexion between touch and sight has been established or how each sense by itself first becomes able to appreciate and interpret its own kind of stimuli. He seems to think that if the eye is normal and gets opportunity for exercise, it cannot help seeing, just as the ear or the nose cannot help hearing or smelling. [3] The reason for this is perhaps to be found in the fact that all through the analysis of mind in the *Essay* he is dealing with the adult, and so is able to take the existence of the mature forms of sense activity

[1] Book II, ch. i. 23. *Cf.* ch. iii. of the same Book.
[2] Book II, ch. ix. 8, 9.
[3] Book II, ch. i. 6.

for granted without needing to consider the conditions determining their genesis and improvement. The result of this assumption is that when he comes to speak of the education of the child he makes the common mistake of crediting him with capacities like those of the adult, and the necessity for ensuring a right training in the use of those senses without which there could be no knowledge of any kind escapes his attention altogether.

But though Locke generally makes a sharp distinction between the care of the body and the culture of the mind and ignores the need for a specific training of the senses, the medical and the pedagogical views occasionally come together, almost in spite of his effort to keep them apart. There is one passage, for example, which appears to be only a casual utterance, and which yet is full of significance as an indication of the trend of Locke's thought. " There are not more differences in men's faces and the outward lineaments of their bodies," he says, " than there are in the makes and tempers of their minds." [1] No attempt is made to suggest a connexion between the differences of body and the differences of mind. At the same time, it is to be noted, the variations of individuality which are conspicuous and unmistakable on the physical plane are made the key to the appreciation of individuality in mind and character. When men's

[1] Section 101.

bodies are so different, he argues, it is difficult to imagine that their minds are the same ; and straightway there disappears the notion of a standard kind of mind with a stock equipment of faculties, which is apt to be derived from an exaggerated insistence on the opposition of body and mind, and which would not be inconsistent with Locke's own doctrine of mind as initially a *tabula rasa* on which the educator makes what impressions he will. It is obvious that if minds are as diverse as bodies, the same individual consideration must be given to the one as to the other. " Each man's mind," as Locke says, " has some peculiarity as well as his face that distinguishes him from all others ; and there are possibly scarce two children who can be conducted by exactly the same method." [1] Consequently the teacher, like the doctor, must renounce universal specifics and treat each case on its merits.

Here Locke states quite explicitly and practically for the first time the principle of educational individualism which has been the watchword of all progress in education from his day to ours. Most previous educators had worked on the assumption that education is a more or less uniform process in which the same subjects taught in the same way would produce the same cultural effect ; and even those before Locke who were dissatisfied with the traditions of the Renaissance which had

[1] Section 216.

become stereotyped in the practice of the schools and universities had no exact idea of their essential defect, and generally thought to find a remedy in a mere change of subjects and pursuits. Locke, fortunate in combining the experience of a physician with that of a teacher, hit on the truth, almost by accident, that there can be no true education which does not adapt itself to the nature of the learner.

It cannot be said that Locke had any clear notion of the practical consequences of his position. His curriculum of studies, though different in many respects from that generally followed in the homes and schools of his day, is based on adult needs rather than on childish capacities, and is so far inconsistent with his own principles. Nevertheless, his whole discussion of the methods and subjects of instruction has implicit in it the modern conception of education as primarily an individual matter. It is this, for example, which underlies his objections to the wholesale methods of the schools and leads him to prefer the tutorial system. " Let the master's industry and skill be never so much," he insists, " it is impossible he should have fifty or a hundred scholars under his eye any longer than they are in school together ; nor can it be expected that he should instruct them successfully in anything but their books ; the forming of their mind and manners requiring a constant attention and particular application to every single boy, which is impossible in a numerous flock." [1]

Even more notable is his clear and emphatic statement of the need for freedom as the vital condition of a true education. "Children," he says in a passage which shows as definite an appreciation of the juvenile point of view as any in modern educational literature, "have as much a mind to show that they are free, that their own good actions come from themselves, that they are absolute and independent, as any of the proudest of you grown men." [2] "As a consequence of this," he goes on, "they should seldom be put upon doing even those things you have an inclination in them to, but when they have a mind and disposition to it." This method of liberty has two great advantages. In the first place it makes for the most profitable kind of study. Locke appeals to adult experience in confirmation of this. He points out that the man who loves reading or music finds occasionally that he is not in the mood for them, and that if he forces himself to turn his attention to them he wearies himself to no purpose. It is the same, he maintains, with children. For them also there are times and seasons when work is done easily, and if these are utilized learning ceases to give them any trouble. "By this means a great deal of time and tiring would be saved ; for the child will learn three times

[1] Section 70.   [2] Section 73.

as much when he is in tune as he will with double the time and pains when he goes awkwardly or is dragged unwillingly to it. And if things were ordered aright, learning anything they should be taught might be made as much a recreation to their play as their play is to their learning." [1] It is a further advantage of the method that the teacher gets the opportunity of knowing his pupil's character thoroughly and is able to deal with him in the way best suited to his case. Suppose, says Locke, the boy is prone to saunter (or, as we would say, to ' dawdle '). It is important to ascertain whether this is a natural infirmity or a moral defect, because the treatment called for in the two cases is quite different. Such facts are only to be found out by careful observation of the boy when he is left free to follow his own bent and he supposes himself not to be under supervision. Under these conditions he will reveal his true character, and the teacher will have no difficulty in moulding and fashioning him as he pleases.

BIBLIOGRAPHICAL NOTE

Some Thoughts concerning Education has been edited by Evan Daniel (London, 1880), and by R. H. Quick (Cambridge, 1880) ; and *The Conduct of the Understanding* by T. Fowler (Oxford, 1880). *The Educational Writings of John Locke*, edited by J. W. Adamson (London, 1912), gives both works in slightly abridged form.

[1] Section 74.

CHAPTER II

ETIENNE BONNOT DE CONDILLAC

1715–1780

IN the *Essay concerning Human Understanding*
Locke followed Descartes in emphasizing the
twofold origin of knowledge in outer and inner
experience, in sensation and reflection. But as he
made reflection entirely dependent on sensation
both for its occasion and for its content, it is not
surprising that most of his followers set aside the
doctrine of the incorporeality and independence of
mind and transformed his philosophy into some
sort of sensationalism. This reshaping of Locke's
ideas took many different forms, of which the most
immediately influential in the sphere of education
was undoubtedly that of Etienne Bonnot de
Condillac, the member of a noble French family,
and titular Abbé de Mureaux.[1]

Voltaire in his *Letters on the English* presented

---

[1] Windelband gives an admirable account of the several lines along
which Locke's philosophy divagated in its various developments
(*History of Philosophy*, Eng. trans., pp. 450–462). In view of the
fact that 'physiological education' is in large measure the result of
applying medical methods of thought to education, it is interesting to
note—what Windelband brings out very clearly—how considerable
was the part played by philosophically minded physicians in working
out the sensationalist implications of Locke's thought.

Etienne Bonnot de Condillac

Locke to the French public in the most sensationalist guise. Condillac, following up Voltaire, developed the associational psychology still further, and explicitly set aside the idea of mental activity of any kind as an original factor in experience. According to the view which he presented with great ingenuity and with much literary skill in his *Traité des Sensations*, the one essential attribute of mind is its capacity for sensation. Even the combinations of the various ideas that come through the senses are but sensations : sensations present together in the same consciousness give rise to the new sensations of their relation. Nothing more is needed to explain the most complex ideas or the mental operations they imply. In demonstration of this, he shows with the help of the naïve fiction of a statue which began with a single sense and afterwards acquired all the others, how the whole of human knowledge and conduct is gradually built up from the various sense-impressions.

In such a psychology as this the senses inevitably come in for very considerable attention, and it might be expected that they would also bulk largely in any scheme of education based upon it. But, with curious inconsistency, when Condillac turned educator he paid no more attention to the training of the senses than Locke had done. When he published his *Essay on the Origins of Human Knowledge* in exposition and defence of Locke he was not even aware of the need for training them. It was only after a time that the significance of his master's account of the man born blind who had received his sight became evident to him, and he realized that it is not a matter of course that the eye should be able to distinguish the shapes, sizes, positions, and distances of objects. Even then, when he set himself in his *Treatise on the Sensations* to show that the senses only furnish knowledge after they have been trained by experience, he stated his case apologetically, as though the view he was enunciating was sure to encounter popular disbelief: " To say that we have learned to see, hear, taste, feel, and touch appears utterly paradoxical. It looks as if Nature gave us complete use of our senses at the very instant she formed them." [1] In the introductory sections of a thirteen-volume Course of Instruction which he prepared for Louis XV's grandson, the Prince of Parma, to whom he acted as tutor for several years, the initial impotence of the senses is again pointed out and it is recognized that some preparation for their use is necessary. But he soon makes it plain that he does not consider this training of the senses a matter for the educator at all. He assumes that whatever training they require will come in the course of infant experience through the cultivation of the faculty of reasoning. " We only know what we have learned," he says.

[1] i. 2, 3.

Etienne Bonnot de Condillac

" We judge objects by touch, for example, only because we have learned to judge. In effect, since the size of an object depends on its relations to other objects, we must compare it with other objects and judge whether it differs from them by less or more if we are to form an idea of its size. . . . It is the same with ideas of distance, of shape, and of weight. In a word, all the ideas that come to us through touch presuppose comparisons and judgments. No sooner is touch trained than it becomes the teacher of the other senses. It is from it that the eyes, which by themselves would only have sensations of light and colour, learn to estimate sizes, forms, and distances ; and they are trained so quickly that they seem to see without having learned. . . . It is proved, then," he adds, " that the faculty of reasoning appears as soon as our senses begin to develop ; and that we have the use of our senses at an early age, only because we have reasoned at an early age." [1]

The practical deductions from this view are interesting. To all intents and purposes, " the faculties of the understanding are the same in a child as in a grown-up man." The main difference between man and child is in the extent of their experience and knowledge. Consequently there is no truth of any kind which is beyond the child's comprehension, if only he is led up to it by proper gradations. Instead of spending time in the training

[1] i. 47–49.

of the senses, then, Condillac attempted to give his seven-year-old pupil a training in observation and reasoning. After a preliminary course in personal psychology to acquaint the boy with what was happening in his own mind when he was being educated and to enable him to co-operate with his teacher, he sought to make him reflect on the origins of society so that he might traverse for himself the road followed by humanity in the creation of the arts and sciences and develop the faculty of reasoning in the process. Thereafter he led him on to the study of various branches of learning.

There is no need to dwell further on these curious proposals of Condillac or to discuss their implications. They have but slight practical value, and have only been mentioned to show how little Condillac realized the educational applications of his own psychology. It is not to them that he owes his place in the history of educational theory, but to the fact that he advanced beyond Locke in the clearer apprehension of the need for some training for *all* the senses. Even though this idea was rendered sterile in his own practice by the assumption that no sense training is necessary beyond what the child gets through his infantile reasoning, it made possible the development of the more fruitful conceptions of the place of the senses in the intellectual life which found their first expression in Rousseau (a close student of the *Treatise on the*

Etienne Bonnot de Condillac

Sensations), and through him have exercised a profound influence on all modern thought about education.

BIBLIOGRAPHICAL NOTE

The *Essai sur l'Origine de la Connaissance humaine* was published in 1746, and the more important *Traité des Sensations* in 1754 (eight years before the publication of the *Emile*). The *Cours d'Etude pour l'Instruction du Prince de Parme* appeared in 1775.

CHAPTER III

JACOB RODRIGUEZ PEREIRA

1715–1780

THE eighteenth century saw a notable advance in the education of deaf-mutes. Many attempts had been made to overcome the difficulty of teaching these unfortunates in individual cases during the course of the previous century, but it was not till the middle of the eighteenth century that institutions were established for the systematic treatment of them and methods similar to those now employed first tried with a number of pupils. The Abbé de l'Epée in France, Thomas Braidwood in Scotland, Samuel Heinicke in Germany share the honours of this advance.[1] But rather earlier than any of these, and of greater significance for the development of the idea of a physiological education, was Jacob Rodriguez Pereira, the pioneer of this work in France. Pereira was a Spanish Jew of Portuguese origin. Coming to Bordeaux at the age of eighteen in pursuance of his business, he became acquainted with a young woman who had been dumb from birth. His affection for her led him to devote himself from that

[1] See Monroe's *Cyclopedia of Education*, ii. 257, for details.

Jacob Rodriguez Pereira

time to the discovery of means for making deaf-mutes speak. To qualify himself for his self-appointed task, he went through a special medical course, and subsequently undertook the education of several pupils. His first definite success was achieved with a Jewish boy of thirteen, whom he taught by dint of patient effort not only to name the letters of the alphabet, but also to articulate some common phrases. Four years later (in 1749) he presented another pupil to the Academy of Sciences in Paris, and received the commendations of Buffon[1] and the other academicians on the committee appointed to examine his methods. Their eulogy brought him to the notice of Louis XV, who conferred a pension on him " in consideration of the art acquired by him of being able to teach deaf-mutes to speak." He instituted a free school in Bordeaux in 1750, but transferred it to Paris two or three years later. Deaf-mutes came to this school from all parts of Europe, and there were generally from ten to fifteen children under his care. In 1759 he was elected a member of the Royal Society of London. The closing years of his life were spent in obscurity, and he died in 1780.

It is not easy to get any very clear account of his methods and principles. Early in his career he invented a ' Dactylologie,' a system of some

---

[1] *Cf.* Buffon's *Natural History*, xii. 155, 156.

forty signs requiring the use of only one hand. But finding the credit he thought due to his invention appropriated by the Abbé de l'Epée, he took pains to prevent the more valuable oral method, by which he made his pupils able to speak and to understand speech, from becoming public property, and carried his secret with him to the grave.[1]

But the researches of Seguin have recovered the general principles if not the details of his method. To begin with, he got into touch with his pupils by means of a manual alphabet devised by a Spaniard named Bonet and his own system of syllabic signs. As soon as he succeeded in making them understand him, he proceeded to teach them to speak by a method in which lip-reading played a prominent part. His problem, we are told, was this : " Given a deaf-mute, to make him understand speech and to teach it to him through vision, so that (1) he will watch people speaking and see by the movements of articulation what they are expressing by the voice ; (2) he himself will articulate his thought as he sees other people doing it ; (3) and consequently, though he remains deaf, he will not be wholly without the faculty of speech, but will see the words he does not hear and find himself

---

[1] So Itard, *Traité des Maladies de l'Oreille*, ii. 472. Politzer, however, is of opinion that he was merely an empiric, and had no secret method (*Geschichte der Ohrenheilkunde*, i. 429).

on an equal footing with speaking and thinking humanity."

But there seems to have been more than lip-reading in his method. We are informed on good authority that he produced in his pupils not only a natural voice and a correct pronunciation, but even his *accent gascon*, or peculiar Southern intonation. The secret is perhaps to be found in what Seguin calls a 'physiological discovery': "Pereira analysed the speech into two elements: the sound and the vibration which produces it; the first which the ear alone can perceive, the second that any flesh vibrating itself may be taught to perceive. He conceived that ordinary men hear the sound without, most of the time, noticing the vibrations; but that the deaf who cannot hear the sound may nevertheless be made the recipients of the vibrations. Hence, a given vibration producing only a given sound, the deaf taught to perceive the vibration could not imitate it without reproducing likewise the corresponding sound of language. It is thus that he practically made his pupils hear through the skin and utter exactly what they so heard. By this discovery, Pereira demonstrated to the physiologists of his day that all the senses are modifications of the tact, all touch of some sort." [1]

[1] Compare with this a striking passage in an article on *The Education of the Deaf-blind* in Monroe's *Cyclopedia of Education*, ii. 267, by

From Locke to Montessori

This statement of the fundamental principles of Pereira's practice is somewhat vague. But Seguin seems to be right in finding implicit in it the central ideas of a physiological education based on sense-training. The conclusions indicated by Pereira's experiments, according to him, are these : (1) That the senses, and each one in particular, can be submitted to physiological training by which their primordial capacity may be indefinitely intellectualized. (2) That one sense may be substituted for another as a means of comprehension and of intellectual culture. (3) That the physiological exercise of one sense corroborates the action as well as verifies the acquisitions of another. (4) That our most abstract ideas are comparisons and generalizations by the mind of what we have perceived through our senses. (5) That educating the modes of perception is to prepare pabulum for the mind proper. (6) That sensations are intellectual functions performed through external apparatus as

Miss Sullivan, the teacher of Helen Keller : "Not enough emphasis has been put on the sense of touch, which is the great sense. The whole skin sees and listens, and not only the skin but the entire body, bones and muscles. Psychologically, and as a matter of biological history, hearing and sight are only specializations of the sense of touch, and, as the parent of these senses, it has many capacities which in normal people have been appropriated by the finer offspring : these capacities are still available in the redemption of the deaf-blind from idiocy. Through them by tactual experience of the outer world, combined with a language which is instinct with the wisdom of the race, the twice-buried mind can know the sun, the sea, and the stars." *Cf.* also Helen Keller, *The World I live in*, chaps. iv., v.

much as reasoning, imagination, etc., through more internal organs.

If Seguin means to suggest that all this was clearly before Pereira's mind, he is reading too much into his methods. Pereira was certainly not a mere empiricist content to get results without comprehension of their meaning, and it is quite possible that he may have had some notion of the relation between the senses and the higher powers of mind. But his prime concern was the invention of ways and means to make good the defect of the deaf-mute by finding some equivalent for hearing in the other senses. And his main contribution to educational theory is to be found, in the first place, in his recognition that the fundamental position of touch among the senses makes possible the substitution of a touch-mediated experience when the other senses are imperfect or lacking; and, in the second place, in the discovery of how much can be done to train touch to become an instrument ministering to the whole mental life.

There is no reason to think, however, that he had any clear consciousness of the wider implications of his method. It was Rousseau and not Pereira who first realized the possibility of giving to each and every sense the kind of training which Pereira gave to touch, and who extended to the education of normal children the principles on which was based the education of the deaf-mutes. But it was his

From Locke to Montessori

association with Pereira which made this possible. By a fortunate chance, the two men were near neighbours and good friends, and Rousseau was a frequent visitor at the little school in the Rue de la Platrière. Pereira's theories evidently impressed him very deeply, and when he came to work out his own educational plans in the *Emile* a few years later, the influence of Pereira showed itself plainly in his constructive proposals for the education of boyhood.[1]

BIBLIOGRAPHICAL NOTE

For biographical details Larousse's *Dictionnaire du 19e Siècle* and *La Grande Encyclopédie* should be consulted. The most valuable source of information about Pereira's work and principles is Seguin. He wrote a memoir, *Jacob Rodrigue Péreire : Notice sur sa Vie et ses Travaux* (1847), and there are detailed references in his *Traitement Moral, Hygiène, et Education des Idiots* (1846), pp. 325–331, and *Idiocy* (1866), pp. 22–26.

[1] It is overstating the case to say, as Seguin does, that "the book of *Emile* is full of experiments on physiological teaching, which could only have originated in the school for deaf-mutes," but there can be no question that Rousseau owed a good deal to Pereira. This is most evident in the section of *Emile* relating to the training of touch. See, for example, ii. p. 103 (Everyman edition): " As touch when trained takes the place of sight, why should it not to some extent take the place of hearing, seeing that sounds set up vibrations in sonorous bodies, which are appreciable by touch? By placing the hand on the body of a violoncello, one can distinguish without the help of eye or ear, merely by the way in which the wood vibrates and trembles, whether the sound given out is sharp or flat, and whether it is drawn from the treble string or the bass. If only our touch were trained to note these differences, I do not doubt but that in time we might become so sensitive as to hear a whole tune with our fingers."

Jacob Rodriguez Pereira

Pereira himself recorded *Observations sur les Surds et Muets* in the *Recueil des Savants étrangers* (1769). The only other writing of his is a brief *Dissertation sur l'Articulation de l'Insulaire d'Otahiti*, appended to Bougainville's *Voyage autour du Monde*, which is chiefly of value in disproving the charge of empiricism sometimes brought against him.

CHAPTER IV

JEAN JACQUES ROUSSEAU

1712–1778

LIKE most of his contemporaries Rousseau came under the influence of Locke, but, following his fellow-countryman Bonnet [1] rather than Voltaire, he developed the master's philosophy in a form antagonistic to the prevailing sensationalism. He was so far in agreement with Condillac and the Encyclopædists that he attributed the whole content of thought to the senses, but, keeping closer to Locke's original teaching than they, he insisted on the mind's reaction to its sense-experience as an essential element in all knowledge and conduct. The senses, he maintained, give us facts singly and separately as they exist in nature. It is the intelligence which combines them by the operation of comparison and reasoning into the unity of related experience, and makes knowledge possible at all.

This difference in theory had far-reaching consequences in practice, and nowhere more obviously

---

[1] Charles Bonnet, *Essai de Psychologie, ou Considerations sur les Operations de l'Ame, sur l'Habitude et sur l'Education* (London, 1755). His influence on Rousseau is confined for the most part to psychology. The educational doctrines of the two men have nothing in common.

than in education. Thus while Condillac attributed the whole of a man's ideas to social intercourse, and Helvetius, carrying the doctrine of the original blankness of mind a stage further, asserted that whatever differences there are between one man and another are entirely due to education, Rousseau regarded the distinctive nature of the learning mind as the fundamental datum in the process of education. The mind, he says, only produces ideas on the occasion of its sensations, but the manner of its activity does not depend on its sensations, but on itself. It is like the plant which grows well or ill according to the chances of soil and climate, but yet succeeds in some fashion in developing and revealing in mature form the characters which were latent in it from the beginning. Its potentialities may be more or less perfectly realized in different environments, but potentiality is always more than environment. The educator, on this view, is not the master of mind, but its servant. He helps from without a process of growth which has its impulses from within, and only succeeds when he understands and respects its laws.[1]

This is substantially the doctrine stated vaguely and hesitatingly by Locke, that education can only be effective when adapted to the learner ; but

---

[1] *Emile*, i. 5–7. (The references throughout this chapter are to the Everyman edition, but when quotations are made I give my own translation.)

whereas in Locke the reference to the internal factors in education was casual, here it is fundamental. It is not the curriculum of studies or the arts of instruction which are regarded as the central interest of the educator, but the original nature of the learning mind and the manner of its reaction on what it is taught. In thus emphasizing the personal elements in education, Rousseau does for education what Locke himself had done for philosophy : he compels a transfer of attention from knowledge to the process of knowing. He forces the teacher to begin by understanding the child whom he proposes to teach.

With this change of focus new problems immediately come into sight. If, as Rousseau asserts, education ought to be suited to the nature of the child, it is imperative that the educator should know quite definitely what is the nature of the child. This is a question of fact, which Rousseau, in the spirit of his age, approaches from the biological side. An education in accordance with nature means for him primarily an education in accordance with human nature. In his view, there are certain basic dispositions or impulses, characteristic of humanity, which manifest themselves in diverse ways as soon as man enters into relation with the world around him, and which continue to give a distinctive character to all his experiences at the different stages of his mental development. Under the educative pressure of social life, these potencies get some kind of actuality, good or bad : tendencies to act in particular ways become transformed into habits, more or less adequate, of acting in particular ways. The ideal education is one that does fullest justice to all these innate possibilities of human nature. In real life they are apt to be distorted out of all recognition, or even crushed out altogether. Society generally makes the citizen by spoiling the man.

But an education in accordance with nature means more than this for Rousseau. Human nature is not a bloodless abstraction. It always incarnates itself in individual men and women ; and a natural education needs to take this into account. It must adapt itself to the innate dispositions due to sex, which, though expressions of the deepest possible differences within humanity, are yet as fundamental in their own way as the primary human characters. It must adapt itself to the modifications of mind and character which have their origins in the natural process of individual growth, and give to each age a nurture different from that of every other age. It must adapt itself to the infinite variety of individual difference, and deal with every person as a being who with all the common features of race, sex, and age has yet a nature of his own that distinguishes him from every other human being.[1]

---

[1] For the development of these ideas I must refer to my *Educational Theory of Jean Jacques Rousseau*, pp. 156–162, 235 *seq*.

From Locke to Montessori

The comparison of the educative process with organic growth, which is the basis of Rousseau's view of a proper education, furnished him and his successors, Pestalozzi and Froebel, with a great wealth of new ideas, and created a mighty movement of educational regeneration which has not exhausted its strength even yet. The guiding principle of this movement is the principle of freedom. Locke, with sound instinct but with no obvious philosophical justification for his conviction, indicated the value of liberty as a condition of effective learning. Rousseau, seeing in education the evolution of innate powers and emphasizing the personal reaction on experience as against its external elements, extended Locke's doctrine far beyond its original limits and made it the inspiration of a new conception of education.

Man, he declared in the famous epigram with which the *Social Contract* opens, is born free. Freedom is his essential attribute as man. The natural man, who alone is completely man, is the one " who does not allow himself to be drawn away by the passions or opinions of his fellows, who sees with his own eyes and feels with his own heart, who is subject to no other authority than that of his own reason." [1] If through social restraints or coercions of any kind one loses this native freedom and acts wholly at the dictate of another he becomes less

[1] *Emile*, iv. 217.

truly man. The best education, therefore, must have as its ideal to bring about the development of the original nature in such fashion that under all the passing changes of external circumstance the man is impelled to action by no other will than his own. How is this to be effected? Only by a method of education that permits a well-regulated liberty from the beginning. If, as Rousseau is firmly convinced, the prime impulses of human nature are always good and capable of being converted into good actions, the obvious course for the teacher to follow is to provide opportunities for the gradual formation of the habit of self-determined action and to refrain from forcing on the pupil a way of life, however good, which has not the sanction of his own personality.

This principle of pedagogical freedom is not easy to state without dangerous ambiguity. It is not always possible to distinguish in practice between the freedom that consists in obedience to a law which one accepts and imposes on oneself and the freedom that consists in mere revolt against all law; nor to prevent the regulation of impulse without which impulse itself would be a tyranny, passing into a foreign restriction on essential movements of the soul. But though Rousseau sometimes confuses freedom and caprice, and does not always do justice to social institutions which, with all their defects, interpret and fulfil the elemental needs of human nature, his proclamation of the gospel of free development marks the beginning of a new epoch in educational thought and practice. Even if he himself did little to solve the problems involved in the demand for the free education of freemen, he laid them as a burden on the consciences of all later educators.

In working out his scheme for a natural education in the *Emile* Rousseau was forced to construct a genetic psychology for himself. If each age and state of life has its own proper perfection and maturity, the work of education can only be performed in a scientific way by the teacher who knows the distinctive features of his pupil's mental life, and for that purpose the ordinary psychology based on an analysis of the adult mind has only a limited value. There is needed a psychology of boyhood and of youth as well as a psychology of manhood. In dealing with this problem, in the absence of guidance from previous thinkers, Rousseau adopted a simple but effective principle. Like Locke, he distinguished those elements of experience received passively through the senses from those contributed by the mind's own activities in the elaboration of sensations. The latter, he said, are only present in the adult. In infancy the mind is purely passive, and depends for all its knowledge on what comes into it from the world around it. Hence the mental development of every individual is simply the process of transition from sense to intellect, from emotions and images unqualified by memory and reasoning to interrelated ideas created by the mind out of its primary data.

It is a crude view of mind, which it is not possible for any post-Kantian psychologist to accept ; and it is apt to suggest the mischievous doctrine that education should commence on the physical plane and change more or less abruptly to the mental. But in working out its practical applications Rousseau gradually modifies and corrects it. He begins by saying that the boy has images but not ideas, as though the mind were not yet operative in boyhood. But as he goes on he discovers the impossibility of maintaining the opposition of sense passivity and ideational activity, and tacitly recognizes that the higher faculties of mind, on which depends the existence of ideas, are all present already in some form in the first sensory experiences. Even if the developed reason of manhood has not yet appeared in the child, there is present in the seeming passivity of early mind a reason of the senses which anticipates and prepares for the later reason of manhood.[1]

The sharp distinction between functions of mind conditioned by the physical organism and higher functions of an incorporeal kind is not maintained by him even with regard to early childhood, in which

[1] *Emile*, ii. 90, 122.

if anywhere the passivity of mental and the activity of physical life might be expected to be most evident. He does insist that the principle of self-activity confines its manifestations to physical forms at this stage and only enters the sphere of intellect in the pre-adolescent years. But the effects of bodily movements, which are the first self-activities, begin to be felt in the development of mind almost at once. "At the commencement of life, when memory and imagination are as yet inactive, the child limits his attention to what actually affects his senses. He wants to touch and handle everything. Do not check his restlessness. This is a necessary part of his training. It is by looking, fingering, and hearing, and above all by comparing sight and touch, that he learns to feel the heat and cold, the hardness and softness, the heaviness and lightness of bodies, and to judge of their size and form and all their physical properties." The larger movements of the body have also definite mental effects. "It is only by movement that we learn that there are things other than ourselves; and only by our own movements that we get the idea of space." [1]

In this passage we find suggested some of the most characteristic of Rousseau's ideas about early education : its beginning with life itself, the need for a training in the most elementary distinctions of

---

[1] *Emile*, i. 31.

sense-experience, the part played by the body, both in its gross activities and in the adjustments of the senses. But it is not till he comes to discuss the education of the ten-year-old boy in the second book of the *Emile* that their full significance is revealed. Commencing with the conception of the boy's mind as essentially passive, or at any rate as only active when dealing with sense-given objects—both views are to be found in this book—he demonstrates the futility of all the ordinary subjects of instruction for boys. History, geography, literature, languages, deductive mathematics, all err by making an appeal to the reason which has not yet matured. What a blunder it is to turn the boy away from his proper interests in the world immediately around him to these abstract studies! Nature is far wiser in this than we are. The first natural movements of the child lead him to measure himself with his environment and make him eager to experience all the physical qualities of the objects he sees that have any bearing on his own life. " When the delicate and flexible bodily organs are capable of adapting themselves to the objects on which they are to act and the senses are unspoiled and free from illusions, then is the time to exercise them both in their proper business, and to get a knowledge of the physical relation between ourselves and the world. Since everything that comes into the human understanding enters through the senses, the first reason of man is a reason of the senses. It is this that serves as a basis for the reason of intellect. Our first teachers of science are our feet, our hands, and our eyes. . . . To learn to think, therefore, we must exercise the limbs, senses, and organs, which are the instruments of our intellect." [1] Away with books and all the artificial concerns of the schoolroom! Keep the boy in touch with his immediate world and train his body. The intellect will develop as a matter of course. For strength of body calls for free movements of all sorts, and the need for constant adjustment to the various objects around him compels him to behave intelligently and to acquire the only kind of reason of which he is capable. All that is necessary to produce this result is that he should be left free to follow his own devices and allowed to profit by his own experiences without the teacher intervening to do his thinking for him. He will learn more from his play than from any teacher. Lessons that scholars get from each other in the playground are a hundred times more useful to them than all they are ever taught in the class-room.

But while it is true in a general way that every increment of strength, if left free to expend itself, gives a fresh opportunity for intelligent action at an age when intelligent thought is still not to be expected, too much importance must not be attached

[1] *Emile*, ii. 90.

to mere strength. There are forms of physical
training of a mechanical kind which serve to make
the body strong without producing any improvement in the judgment : such, for example, as
swimming, running, leaping, whipping a top or
throwing stones. These are good enough in their
way, but after all we have more than arms and legs.
We have eyes and ears, which need to be trained
if we are to have proper command of our bodies
and to behave intelligently in our relations with our
physical environment. The great movements come
to us naturally. The senses have to be educated.
" We cannot touch, see, or hear unless we have been
taught." Fortunately, boyhood is the nascent
period of the senses. " The senses are the first
faculties to take form and attain perfection, so
that it is right that they should be the first to be
cultivated." [1] This and not book-learning ought
to be the main education of boyhood.

But what is involved in the training of the senses ?
It is not merely using our senses, says Rousseau.
It is learning to judge properly by their means.
Suppose, for example, there is a stream to be
crossed and the question arises whether a plank is
long enough to reach from one side to the other.
The man with a trained eye has only to look at
the breadth of the stream and the length of the
plank, and immediately he knows by an intuitive

[1] *Emile*, ii. 97.

comparison whether the plank is too short or not. Again, take the practical problem of moving a mass with a lever. A person accustomed to the task chooses a pole of the proper length at once and applies it to the best advantage, all without need of deliberate calculation. At eighteen, as Rousseau remarks, we learn in the science class what a lever is ; but there is not a peasant boy of twelve who cannot make better use of a lever than the cleverest mechanician of the Academy. The training of the senses, then, does not merely mean making them more acute in the appreciation of particular sensations, though that no doubt is involved in it. It means the acquisition of the ability to discriminate between the objects that produce the sensations in us, so that we feel with exactness what we do feel and are able to interpret it correctly in objective terms by an immediate judgment.

In this kind of discrimination ordinary experience provides a certain amount of training. We are always using our senses, and with the use of them our proficiency in sense-judgment increases. But there are limits to the degree of this proficiency beyond which untutored experience cannot go. Even in the case of touch, where we have control at a very early age and seem to have little need of training, a comparison of ordinary people with those whose blindness has forced them to rely mainly on

touch shows how much surer and more delicate the
senses may become when they are specially exercised.
It is evident from this that there is plenty of room
for improvement in the senses, and the comparison
suggests the method by which it can be brought
about. We need to concentrate attention on each
sense singly, and provide a special training for it to
make it able to act independently of the other senses.
Consider touch in the first place. In conjunction
with the muscular sense, it brings us into relation
with the various bodies around us which are likely
to affect our own body. It acquaints us with their
heat, their size, their form, their weight, their solidity.
But though it is in constant use every hour of our
waking life, it remains the crudest and least perfect
of all the senses, because we are continually con-
fusing its judgments with those of sight. Sight acts
so much more quickly that the mind is apt to dispense with the tardier information derived from
touch. For its proper training, therefore, we must
occasionally isolate it and force ourselves to depend
on it alone. This, as it happens, is not difficult to
do. When the darkness comes on, sight ceases to
be superior to touch and the blind man has the
advantage over the man who can see. Instead of
turning night into day with artificial lights, let us
follow the blind man's example and learn to see with
our finger-tips. Children permitted to play in the
dark with the same freedom as in the light can soon

move about with perfect assurance and are able to distinguish the various objects they encounter. Touch thus separated from sight and hearing and compelled to take its place as the main recipient of sense-impressions acquires far more than normal sensitiveness, and when ordinary conditions are restored it supplements the other senses far more effectively than the untrained touch.

Sight is more difficult to train than touch. The ultimate aim, as before, is to make it self-sufficient ; but the nature of vision compels us to postpone the detachment of sight from the other senses till the mind is more developed. The objects we see owe the form they take for the eye not merely to their actual size and shape, but to their distance from the eye and the position from which they are seen, so that for the accurate perception of them we must take into account both dimension and distance. Hence, to overcome the natural defects of vision, it is necessary in the first instance to follow a method of training the very opposite of that employed in the case of touch. Instead of simplifying the sense-perception by the exclusion of sensations coming through the other senses, it is always advisable to check the appearances of things as they are seen by comparison with what we learn about them from touch, and restrain the precipitate judgments of the eye by the slower and more deliberate tactile judgments. We must learn from the engineers and other workmen to correct our estimates of height, length, depth, and distance by actual measurement, and acquire in this way the same sureness of eye which characterizes them.

There are plenty of ways of getting visual accuracy developed in childhood, by arousing interest in measuring, recognizing, and estimating distances. " Here is a very high cherry-tree. How are we to gather the cherries ? Will the ladder in the barn be sufficient ? There is a very wide stream. How are we to get across it ? Would one of the planks in the yard reach from bank to bank ? We want to fish in the moat from our windows. How many yards of line shall we need ? I want to make a swing between these two trees. Will two fathoms of rope be enough ? I am told that in the other house our room is to be twenty-five feet square. Do you think it will do for us ? Will it be larger than this one ? We are very hungry. Which of these two villages can we reach first to get our dinner ? " [1] If, in everyday cases like these, children are encouraged to use their judgment, especially if they estimate first and measure afterwards, so as to make the eye and not the measuring instrument their main tool, they soon learn to appreciate distance and to take account of perspective.

Drawing introduces a most valuable form of

[1] *Emile*, ii. 105.

From Locke to Montessori

eye-training. Children, who are great imitators, are all eager to draw ; and provided their work is not a copying of other people's drawings—a mere imitation of imitations—but a serious attempt to depict actual objects, there is no more effective way of giving them an intimate knowledge of the dimensions and sizes of things. It is this rather than its æsthetic influence that makes drawing so important in early education. The young pupil who tries to represent accurately what he sees acquires a true eye and a flexible hand. All unconsciously he gets an intuitive insight into the laws of perspective, that enables him to distinguish between the illusive appearance of things and their reality.

A study near akin to drawing, and capable, like it, of extending the child's acquaintance with dimension, is geometry : not, indeed, deductive geometry, which is beyond his comprehension until he comes nearer adolescence, but practical geometry, in which he gets the proof of various serviceable propositions by using his eyes. This geometry, as Rousseau insists, is not an art of reasoning, but an art of seeing. The pupil makes exact figures, combines them, superimposes one on another, examines their relations ; and out of his inspection he gets not merely new knowledge, but (what is more important at the stage he has reached) new power to observe with precision.

For quickness of eye there is no better training

than that which is got from such games of skill
as tennis, archery, ball, and the like. As they
are commonly played, they are adult games,
but there is no reason why they should not be
adapted to the use of children and made to do good
service in cultivating quickness and sureness of
vision.

After dealing in detail with the two senses which
are of most account in ordinary life, Rousseau
contents himself with suggesting that the same
principles which apply to them apply also to hearing,
taste, and smell, and confines his discussion of these
senses to a cursory review of their outstanding
features. It is significant that when he comes to
speak about taste and smell, the two senses relating
to food which correspond respectively to touch and
sight in relation to external objects, he advocates
a limitation rather than an extension of their
functions in the interests of simplicity. He sees
plainly that there is no virtue in developing the
power of sense-discrimination beyond the needs of
the best kind of social life.

After twelve the boy's education enters on a new
phase, and sense-training, though still needed to
make the senses self-sufficient, becomes of minor
interest. Instead of physical activity, which has
supplied most of the motive-power for learning up
to this time, there appears activity of mind. Eager
with curiosity, the boy seeks to connect the sense-

experiences of earlier years into some kind of system and takes the first steps in the direction of science. It is not so much the senses that the educator must give attention to now, but the nascent intellect. And yet the new training is most intimately connected with the old. Even in rising above the senses the boy still moves in a world of sense-given facts and must not be abruptly removed from it. Let us transform our sensations into ideas, says Rousseau, but do not let us leap headlong from objects of sense to objects of intellect.[1] It is still too soon for the mind to occupy itself with abstractions. There should be no book but the world, no instruction but the instruction of facts. There is plenty of time for speculative thought when adolescence comes.

BIBLIOGRAPHICAL NOTE

The only complete English translation of the *Emile* is published in the Everyman Library. There are more or less satisfactory abridgments of it by Payne (International Education Series), Steeg, and Archer (Educational Classics). Selections from the rest of Rousseau's works bearing on education are given in Archer's book, and in my own *Minor Educational Writings of Rousseau*. For a more complete account of Rousseau's doctrines I may refer to my *Educational Theory of Jean Jacques Rousseau*.

Since there has been a very general failure to follow Rousseau's own argument about the training of the senses (shown, for example, by the mutilation of that part of the second book of the *Emile* dealing with the subject in all the

[1] *Emile*, iii. 167–168.

Jean Jacques Rousseau

three English abridgments of the *Emile*), I append a brief analysis of the relevant sections :

> *The propereducation of the boy up to the age of twelve*
> (pp. 88–122).
>
> (*a*) The exercise and culture of the body (pp. 82–97).
>
> (*b*) The training of the senses :
> Introductory (p. 97); touch (pp. 97–104); sight (pp. 104–112); hearing (pp. 112–115); taste (pp. 115–120); smell (pp. 121–122). See also Book III (pp. 167 *et seq.*).

CHAPTER V

JEAN MARC GASPARD ITARD

1775–1838

JEAN MARC GASPARD ITARD was born in 1775 at Oraison, a little town of old Provence. It had been intended that he should enter on a business career, but the outbreak of the French Revolution changed the course of his life. To avoid conscription, when war broke out between France and the rest of Europe, he got temporary employment as an assistant surgeon in a military hospital; and by this chance he discovered his life's vocation. He devoted himself with great zeal to the study necessary for his new profession, and soon gained distinction as an operator. At the age of twenty-five he became physician to the Institution for Deaf-Mutes in Paris. Shortly after his installation there was brought to the institution a boy of eleven or twelve, named by the newspapers of the day the Savage of Aveyron, who had been found running wild in the woods without any human associates. Itard, sharing the general interest of scientists and philosophers in the case, brought all the resources of his ingenious mind to bear on the education of this boy for four years, and achieved a measure of success which won him a European reputation. He subsequently gave himself to the scientific study of the ear, and published in 1821 a masterly *Treatise on the Diseases of the Ear and of Hearing*, which made a notable contribution to the education of the deaf and laid the foundations of modern otiatry. He died in 1838, high in professional honour and in public esteem.

His two reports on the Savage of Aveyron, one written nine months after the beginning of the experiment, the other after its completion five years later, are important documents both for psychology and for education. In the first report he relates the circumstances under which he undertook the treatment of the Savage, and the methods he followed in dealing with him. The boy had been caught in the woods of Aveyron in 1799, and after some months had been brought to Paris to gratify scientific curiosity. For a time men of science came to visit him in considerable numbers, expecting to find in him the much-discussed man of nature and hoping to get some new light on the human mind from the study of him. To their surprise, all they saw was a boy of disgusting habits, swaying unceasingly from side to side like some caged beast, biting and scratching those who thwarted him, showing no signs of affection for his attendants, completely indifferent to all that was going on around him. Naturally enough, the force of public interest was soon spent, and then the unfortunate child was entrusted to the care of the Institution for Deaf-Mutes. What was to be done with him? Dr Pinel, a famous authority on insanity, in a statement made to the Academy of Sciences, gave it as his opinion that the boy was an incurable idiot whom it would be impossible to educate. With respect to his senses, he pointed out, the boy was inferior to the domestic animals. His eyes were utterly lacking in expression and wandered aimlessly from object to object. His ear was insensible both to loud sounds and to music. The sense of smell was so undeveloped that he was equally indifferent to perfumes and foul odours. The organ of touch was only capable of the mechanical functions of grasping. The intellectual faculties were in no better case. Apart from the objects of physical need, he was totally unable to pay attention to anything, and consequently was devoid of memory, judgment, and the aptitude for imitation. He could not open a door or get up on a chair to reach food that had been put out of his reach. He had no means of communication with his fellows. He passed abruptly and without intelligible motive from an apathetic melancholy to immoderate bursts of laughter. His whole existence, in a word, was on a purely animal level.

Itard accepted Dr Pinel's statement of the facts of the case; but with the rashness of youth he refused to accept his conclusion. He was a whole-hearted disciple of Condillac, and it seemed to him that the simplest explanation of the apparent idiocy of the Savage was to be found in the fact that he had always lived outside of society and had never had his faculties trained by education of any kind. If he had taken Pinel's view, he would have proceeded no further with his enterprise; for it was universally believed at that time that it was impossible to educate an idiot. But it seemed to him that the problem presented by the condition of the Savage was one which could be solved by the combination of medical science and philosophy, and he expressed himself hopeful of performing the double task of restoring the faculties of body and mind that had become atrophied with disuse, and of determining with exactness what knowledge and ideas man owes to education.

The case of the Savage undoubtedly presented some new features, but even before this time Willis and Crichton, two English doctors, had extended the scope of medical treatment to some forms of mental defect, and he felt that he had only to work in the spirit of their doctrines to succeed with the education of his own charge. To begin with, he set before himself five main objects: (1) To render social life more congenial to the boy by making it more like the wild life he had but recently left. (2) To awaken the nervous sensibility by the strongest stimuli and by an occasional quickening of the emotions. (3) To extend the range of his ideas by creating new wants and multiplying his relations with the world around him. (4) To lead him to the use of speech by making it imperatively necessary that he should imitate. (5) To exercise the mind for a time on his physical wants, and from that to lead on to the application of his intelligence to the objects of instruction.

(1) The method adopted by Itard to reconcile the boy to his new social life was to give the utmost possible latitude to his primitive impulses. He recognized that he was still a wild creature, ready to be stirred to a fierce joy at the onset of the tempest and the fall of the snow, or to be subdued into a brooding melancholy by the light of the moon ; [1] and that, like the savages with whom he was popularly classed, he was most content when he was sleeping, eating, idling, or running unrestrained in the fields.

---

[1] "One morning when there had been a heavy fall of snow before he got up he woke with a cry of joy, leapt from his bed, ran with impatience first to the window and then to the door, escaped half dressed and reached the garden. Then, venting his joy in the most piercing cries, he rushed about, rolled himself in the snow, and, gathering it with his fists, devoured it with incredible avidity." (P. 14.) "When the rays of the moon came into his room during the night, he rarely failed to awake and post himself at the window. There he remained part of the night, standing motionless, with outstretched neck, his eyes gazing on the country lighted by the moon, his whole being given up to a contemplative ecstasy, which was only broken by a quick breathing at long intervals, almost always accompanied by a plaintive little sound." (P. 15.)

Consequently he made no attempt to check these long-established habits, and in the end he had his reward in seeing the boy gradually give them up and settle down to a more ordinary life.

(2) Itard's own observations more than confirmed Pinel's account of the defective sensibility of the boy. He found him, for example, wholly indifferent to extremes of heat and cold : he could remain exposed half naked to the cold winds and could pick up glowing coals that had fallen from the fire. The ear seemed to be the most obtuse of all the sense organs. He could hear the fall of a nut or any other eatable, but he paid scarcely any attention to a pistol-shot fired immediately behind him. Arguing from the delicate senses of people who live in hot countries, Itard gave him a course of frequent warm baths. By this and other means he succeeded in making touch, taste, and smell more responsive to stimuli, without producing any effect, however, on sight and hearing. From this he concluded that these three senses are modifications of the organ of the skin and differ in character from sight and hearing, which by reason of their greater complexity he regarded as in a class apart.

(3) It proved more difficult than Itard had expected to create any new wants in the boy. Ordinary toys did not appeal to him at all. The only game he learned to play was an after-dinner one, the main feature of which was the finding of a

chestnut hidden under one of three silver vessels. He continued to get amusement from this occupation even after a non-edible article had been substituted for the chestnut. The most definitely human need that developed in him was his desire for the company of the lady who took care of him. He never parted from her without grief, and was correspondingly happy when he met her again. His fondness for Itard, though less pronounced, was equally evident.

(4) The attempt to teach him to speak proved an almost complete failure. He learned to utter a few sounds like 'lait' and other syllables containing the 'l' sound, but in no case with intelligence and desire. The word was associated for him in a vague way with milk, but was sometimes uttered before he got it and sometimes after, and never to express a wish for it. Itard thought that the complete disuse of the ear during the years he had lived alone had made it unfit for its proper functions without a longer training than it had yet got, and that the habit of expressing his wants by gestures, being more immediately effective than his halting attempts at speech, had prevented the acquirement of speech.

(5) After trying in vain by the methods found successful in the education of deaf-mutes to get his pupil to connect printed words with the objects they designated, Itard invented a method of his

own. He pasted a red circle, a blue triangle, and a black square on a board, and gave the boy three pieces of cardboard of the same size, shape, and colour to put on the top of them. When this was learned, the task was varied : sometimes, for example, the difference of colour was eliminated, at other times colours and shapes were differently associated. Then a more complicated exercise was introduced. The boy was given a case with twenty-four compartments, in each of which was a cardboard square with one of the letters of the alphabet printed on it, and along with this a corresponding set of metal letters. He proved unexpectedly quick at sorting out the letters and matching the two sets ; and, what was most gratifying of all to Itard, he finally learned to pick out the letters L A I T and put them down on the table when he wanted milk. At last he had got a glimmering of the relation between word and thing.

When the first report was written Itard was still of the opinion that his pupil did not differ from other boys in any essential respects. No doubt he had none of the ideas that make the difference between civilized man and the animals, and his faculties were all benumbed from lack of exercise. But it did not seem to Itard that there was any inherent defect in him that would prevent him becoming a more or less normal man if he were properly educated. The hope, excited by the success intimated at the end of the first report, however, turned out to be illusory, and the truth was gradually forced on Itard by the facts of the case. He never admitted his mistake in diagnosis in so many words,[1] but the changes he made in the boy's education were significant. The new methods, as Seguin points out,[2] differed from those first tried in being more suited for an idiot than for a savage. They assumed congenital incapacity such as could only be removed by a mental reconstruction beginning on the physiological level with the simplest elements of sense-experience.

The principle which guided Itard in his second course of experiments was the idea, which he refers to Locke and Condillac, of the potent influence exercised on the formation and development of intellect by the isolated and simultaneous action of the senses.[3] This gave him the suggestion of what

---

[1] Thirty years after he published a memoir on *Mutism produced by Lesion of the Intellectual Faculties.* Did he regard the case of the Savage as coming under this category? The only remark in the memoir which might have reference to him is a vague one : "It is because I have been deceived once that I make this reflection." "A naïve and touching avowal," comments Bousquet, "inspired perhaps by the recollection of the Savage of Aveyron. Perhaps, we say, for we have not received his confidences in this matter. Too modest or too severe toward himself, he did not care to recall the beginnings of his career." (Bousquet, *Eloge historique*, p. xviii.)

[2] E. Seguin, *Idiocy*, p. 26.

[3] Seguin in the passage cited above conveys the impression that Itard in framing his second programme was guided by the principles of Pereira and Rousseau. That is wrong. Itard knew very little about Pereira's work (see the *Traité des Maladies de l'Oreille*, ii. 472);

he calls ' a medical education,' and he set himself
whole-heartedly to exercise and improve separately
all the sense organs of his pupil. As hearing, in his
judgment, is the sense which most definitely favours
the development of the intellectual faculties, he
began with a strenuous attempt to reawaken the
long dormant sensibility of the ears. To compel
their activity, he cut off the competing influences of
sight by tying a thick bandage over the boy's eyes.
He then produced in immediate succession two
extremely loud sounds of a sharply contrasted
kind, the sound of a bell and the sound of a drum.
When the boy heard the sound, he had to show
that he knew what it was by making it himself.
Itard's expectation was that just as he had led him
a year before from the broad comparison of pieces
of cardboard of different colour and shape to the
discrimination of letters and words, he would now be
able to get him to pass gradually from the appreciation of well-marked differences in sounds to the
distinction of the various tones of the human voice.
For this reason he sought to make the sounds he
employed progressively less dissimilar. Soon he
was not content to have him distinguish between

and he only once refers to Rousseau—as a ' case,' not as an authority.
The fact is that Itard's philosophical horizon was very narrow. His
one master was Condillac. It should be added that there is an element
of truth in what Seguin says. The views which Itard found in Locke
and Condillac were not really their views, but their views as modified
and developed by later thinkers, and especially by Rousseau.

the bell and the drum, but aimed at getting him to know the different sounds caused by the stroke of the drumstick on various parts of the drum or on the bell of a clock or on a shovel. When he had accomplished this successfully, he repeated the same comparative method with the sounds of a wind instrument, which, being more like the human voice, was intended to lead his pupil up to the hearing of the different intonations of the larynx. Again success crowned his efforts, and he had the satisfaction of finding the ear of his pupil capable of hearing the most feeble sounds of his voice. When this point had been reached the boy himself began to exhibit a most lively pleasure in his exercises, and would often bring the bandage by which he was blindfolded to persuade Itard to give him more lessons. Encouraged by this, Itard now tried to teach him to distinguish the vowel sounds. O was first learned, then A, but the others presented great difficulties. In the end, however, they also were mastered. But this success was achieved at too great a cost. The close attention required seemed to upset the balance of the boy's mind. Every time he managed to respond correctly to the tests he burst into uncontrollable screams of laughter, which threw all his senses into utter confusion and made any further progress impossible. After trying various expedients to overcome this unexpected obstacle, Itard was finally compelled to recognize that nothing further could be done in the training of the ear.

The explanation of this failure is simple enough, and Itard might have found it for himself in the experience of his predecessors, if not in his own. Instead of beginning the education of the senses with touch, the simplest and most elementary, as he would have done if he had followed Buffon and Condillac in this respect, he chose to begin with hearing, one of the most complex. All later attempts at the training of idiots have avoided his error. But he himself never discovered it. Baffled with hearing, he turned to sight, which is also complex, and, following the same method of graded progress in the perception of distinctions, he succeeded in teaching his pupil, after months of labour, to read and to write quite passably a series of words, several of which were so much alike as only to be distinguished by an attentive eye. Apart from the fact that this involved an extension of the power of sense-discrimination to a new sphere, it did not represent any real advance in intelligence. The boy read the words exactly enough, but he did not understand their meaning. Itard, however, was satisfied that some progress had been made, and he proceeded to deal with the sense of touch.

He found that the boy was able to distinguish differences of temperature in the objects he handled, but he confused things like chestnuts and acorns.

To enable him to discern form by means of touch, he put in his hands various objects differing both in shape and volume (such as a halfpenny and a key), and succeeded with some difficulty in teaching him to know them by feeling them. Then, as before, he led him on gradually to deal with less evident differences, until at last he could distinguish metal letters so much alike as B and R, and C and G. These exercises, Itard confesses, had a greater success than he anticipated. They helped considerably to increase his pupil's power of keeping his attention sustained. When he was busy deciding on the difference in the form of bodies submitted to tactual examination his face assumed a calm and meditative look never present at ordinary times.

The other two senses had not the same need of training. It would have been impossible, indeed, to add anything to the delicacy of the boy's sense of smell, which had a keenness and sureness more animal than human. Taste was also quite adequate for the needs of nature, but Itard thought it advantageous to develop it, or rather to ' pervert ' it,[1] to make his pupil capable of enjoying the various articles of food and drink which civilized man has learned to appreciate. In the course of time the

---

[1] This is a curious echo of the Rousselian philosophy, all the more unexpected because Itard without ever referring explicitly to Rousseau generally assumes a hostile attitude to his doctrines (see especially the closing sections of the first report, p. 49).

boy became quite accustomed to the new foodstuffs, but he showed a persistent aversion to all strong alcoholic liquors and continued to drink water with evident pleasure.

The training of the senses was now completed, and, except in the case of hearing, the result, in Itard's opinion, was highly satisfactory. The boy had been taught to distinguish a round body from a flat by touch, a red paper from a blue by sight, an acid liquid from a bland by taste, and at the same time had learned the names corresponding to these different perceptions. But he was still ignorant of the meaning of the words he used. That called for a further education—the education of the intellect. In making this distinction between the sensorial and the intellectual training, however, Itard does not mean to imply that the intellect had not been at work before. On the contrary, as he is careful to point out, the connexion between the physical and the intellectual is so intimate that it is not possible to exercise the senses without at the same time calling all the faculties into play. The perception and discrimination of new objects by the extension of the sensory range necessarily involves attention, comparison, and memory, and is so far a preparation for the higher activities of mind.

With a view to the development of the intellectual functions, Itard now set himself to establish a precise and definite relation between objects and words. As we have seen, he had already made some tentative experiments in this direction with words like 'lait,' referring to food, but he was doubtful how much the words meant for his pupil even when they were used with seeming intelligence. The word 'lait,' for example, appeared to come to the boy's mind only at the sight of milk, and even then might signify the liquid or the vessel containing it or the desire he had for it. To escape from this ambiguity Itard placed several simple objects (a pen, a key, a knife, a box, etc.) on a shelf, with a card underneath each of them on which the name was inscribed. After teaching the boy to connect every object with its name, he put them all together in one corner of the room and sent him to fetch the one for which he gave him the card. This proved a difficult exercise, but gradually the boy became able to do it quite well. The objects were then put in another room, and he was sent to fetch first one, then two, then three, and finally four at a time. Everything appeared to be going smoothly, until one day it occurred to Itard to vary the experiment. He put within easy reach objects similar to those which were usually fetched from the other room, and tried to get him to recognize them. To his utter discomfiture, he discovered that the boy had not the slightest notion of generality. The knife suggested to him by the word was only one particular knife : he could not connect the word with any knives at all different from the one used in the experiment. For the first time Itard despaired of success. "Wretched boy," he said to him, "since my trouble is wasted and your efforts are vain, back you go to the woods and acquire once more the taste for your primitive life ; or if your new needs make you dependent on society, pay the penalty of being of no use to it, and go and die miserably in the Bicêtre." But the despair was only temporary. Soon Itard was ready to face the new problem with new methods that would compel the boy to grasp the identity of like things ; and he found encouragement in the fact that about this time he first saw in him indications of the power of adapting articles to his own purposes. Again the difficulty was overcome, and thereafter the boy made slow but steady progress in the use of language. He learned many new words, he became able to distinguish and apply names to parts within a whole, he acquired an elementary knowledge of the use of adjectives and verbs.

All the while that this was going on he was being taught to write. At first he could not make any mark with the piece of chalk that was given to him. Itard saw that a preliminary training was needed. He taught him to hold himself in the right position for writing, then put a long, pointed stick into his hand and made him imitate his teacher's movements. Only after that had been accomplished were the writing lessons resumed. The result was that at the end of some months the boy was able to copy the words with which he was already acquainted, and subsequently learned to reproduce them from memory in such a way that he could not merely express his wants and ask for the means of satisfying them, but could understand the needs and wishes of other people when these were communicated to him in writing.

But in spite of all this progress there still remained one great defect : the boy could not speak. For more than a year Itard laboured to overcome this incapacity. He had failed before when he tried to make him able to distinguish words by the ear. He tried now to make the eye take the place of the ear by making him attend to the mechanism of the articulation of sounds. But all in vain. After immense but fruitless labour he was compelled to give up the attempt and abandon his pupil to an incurable mutism.

This was bad enough, but worse was still to follow. Itard had looked forward to the coming of the pubertal crisis, hoping that the great uprising of moral energy which is often so potent a factor in the development of mind and character in normal adolescence would bring with it new opportunities for the boy's education. Instead of that, there came a wild storm of passion which produced a complete change in his nature. The gentle-dispositioned

Jean Marc Gaspard Itard.

boy became a youth of strange and uncontrollable temper, passing rapidly from melancholy to anxiety and from anxiety to rage, disgusted with all that had formerly delighted him, and prone to fits of madness in which he tore off his clothes and bit and scratched his governess. Various means were employed to calm his frenzy, but their effect was only temporary. In the end the directors of the Institution were compelled for the sake of the other children under their charge to send him away. He was entrusted to the care of the lady who had looked after him all along, and he lived with her till his death in 1828.

Though the experiment ended in this unhappy fashion, it had not been made in vain. Its comparative success revealed the possibility of educating idiots by a system of medical pedagogy, and led to a beneficent reform in the treatment of those unfortunate beings. Itard himself took no further part in this work, but he found a useful application for the knowledge he had acquired from his work with the Savage in the establishment of a method of physiological education for deaf-mutes. His observation of the children under his care in the Institution had led him to the conclusion that there are very few deaf people whose ears are completely closed to all sounds. Most of them hear to some extent : many of them only very loud sounds like thunder and the explosion of firearms, others again much slighter

F 81

noises. About two-fifths of them, he estimated, are able to hear the tones of the human voice. Unfortunately all of them alike are condemned to lifelong silence in the absence of a special education. Even those who can hear the voice miss too much of what is said to them to understand the meaning of the words spoken, and soon lapse into the same complete dumbness as the others ; and the ear, deprived of the necessary exercise, gradually loses the limited powers it had at first. Arguing from the analogy of the treatment of limbs which have grown feeble when denied opportunities for movement, Itard was persuaded that there was needed in these latter cases a physiological education of the ear to restore the lost sensibility and to enable the imperfect hearing to contribute as much as possible to the understanding of the spoken word.

To give practical effect to this idea, he began a course of experiments in 1805 with six deaf-mute children. First of all he tried to stimulate their power of hearing by means of a series of sounds of decreasing intensity. He began by making them listen blindfold to the resounding tones of a large church bell, and each day he diminished the loudness of the sound, either by making the children go further away or by striking the bell with a muffled stick. When this means of excitement lost its efficacy he performed the exercises in a fresh way with the bell of a clock. He posted the child who was being tested

Jean Marc Gaspard Itard

at a fixed point in a long straight corridor, sounded the bell quite near him, and gradually moved away, continuing to ring the bell until the child indicated by a signal that he could no longer hear it. Day after day he repeated this, until the improvement in hearing shown by the increasing distance at which the sound was heard came to an end. At that stage he stopped the exercise, because no further benefit was likely to be derived from it.

The purpose of this first exercise was to increase the sensibility of the ear. The next thing was to make the children aware of differences in the intensity of the sounds they perceived, by letting them hear sounds which sometimes varied in the degree of loudness and sometimes were all jumbled together. When he had trained the ear to this new mode of perception, he went on to cultivate the sense of the direction of sound, by walking round about them ringing a small bell and making them point to the part of the room from which the sound came. Then he brought this part of his experiment to a successful close with some exercises in musical rhythm. He beat out simple tunes on the drum and made them distinguish between high and low tones produced on the flute.

By these various exercises the ear had been made capable of hearing the human voice, but it had still to be trained to distinguish the elements of the spoken word. That was difficult enough, but once again the method of graded experiences proved sufficient to overcome the difficulty ; and the time had come to teach the children to reproduce the various vowel and consonant sounds for themselves. Here Itard was working at a new problem. Others before him had tried to teach the dumb to speak by making visual observations of the mechanism of speech the sole basis of training. But having restored the ear to its original power and accustomed it to discriminate the tones of the voice, he wanted to combine eye and ear in the learning of speech. It is unnecessary to enter here into the details of his method. It is enough to say that with infinite patience he triumphed over a host of obstacles and finally succeeded in making his pupils able to form all the elementary sounds of which words are composed. They were still a long way from intelligent speech ; but he thought he had only to teach them all the possible combinations of the sounds they had learned to bring his work to a satisfactory conclusion. It turned out that he was wrong. Children who could read quite intelligently utterly failed to learn to speak. There seemed to him to be two reasons for their impotence. Partly it was due to their habit of expressing their thoughts in manual signs and then translating them laboriously into words. Partly it was due to their inability to remember the words they heard if there were very many of them. Further labour served to remove some of the imperfections of their speech, but these particular children, being only an hour a day with Itard and spending the rest of their time with others who did not employ his methods, never learned to speak properly.

Itard was not the man to own defeat. He worked away steadily at his self-appointed task, and appears in the end to have achieved a greater measure of success. Some ten years later he submitted three memoirs on his system to the Government of the day. These seem to have disappeared, but the report made on them by the Academy of Medicine, to which they had been referred, is still extant, and it bears witness to the efficiency of Itard's system. Its main conclusions are thus summed up :

(1) That the education which consists in the combination of manual signs with speech is possible in the case of one-tenth of the children admitted into the Institution for Deaf-Mutes.

(2) That this education has the advantage of improving the sense of hearing to the point of enabling the pupil to hear one part of the word, to make out with the eyes the part that is not heard, and to complete by means of intelligence and judgment the part which can neither be perceived by ear nor judged by sight.

(3) That in consequence of the various improvements resulting from this special education, the deaf-

mute can . . . converse orally, and receive orders as well as give account of his actions.

(8) That the definite result of this special education would be to return to their families a tenth or a twelfth of the children, able to speak a language which would be understood and by means of which there would consequently be established free, easy, and reciprocal communication, a thing which is impossible when only gesture language is used.

The Commission concluded by expressing the opinion that a class ought to be formed at the Institution for Deaf-Mutes in which children could learn to speak by the method advocated by Itard. It is satisfactory to add that immediate effect was given to this recommendation.

BIBLIOGRAPHICAL NOTE

The most valuable source of information about Itard's life is the *Eloge historique* of A. Bousquet, delivered to the Paris Academy of Medicine the year after his death. None of the articles in the encyclopædias, etc., except that in Hirsch's *Lexikon der Aerzte*, adds many details to those given by Bousquet. Itard's *Rapports et Mémoires sur le Sauvage de l'Aveyron* have been republished in the *Bibliothèque d'Education Spéciale* (Paris, 1894). This edition contains, in addition to the *Rapports et Mémoires*, Bousquet's *Eloge historique*, an *Appréciation* of the *Rapports* by Delasiauve, a *Mémoire sur le Mutisme produit par le Lésion des Fonctions intellectuelles* by Itard himself, and a report by M. Husson on three memoirs by Itard entitled *De l'Education physiologiques du Sens auditif*

Jean Marc Gaspard Itard

chez les Sourds-muets. The account of the later experiments of Itard given in this chapter is based on his *Traité des Maladies de l'Oreille et de l'Audition*, ii. 479–522. It is necessary to add that the statements made by Dr Montessori about Itard's work are in most cases erroneous. There is one dreadful paragraph in *The Montessori Method* (p. 33) where every definite statement made is completely wrong.

CHAPTER VI

EDOUARD SEGUIN

1812–1880

EDOUARD SEGUIN, 'the Apostle of the Idiot,' was born at Clamecy, in France, in 1812. He studied medicine and surgery under Itard, and was encouraged by him to devote himself to the investigation and treatment of idiocy. But though the suggestion for his life-work came both directly and indirectly from Itard, and though the precedent of the education of the Savage of Aveyron was of the utmost value to him, he was not, properly speaking, a disciple of Itard. Itard helped to set him his problem. The guiding ideas which provided him with the solution for it came from Saint-Simon and the Saint-Simonians.

Saint-Simonism, in the form in which it influenced Seguin and many others of the ablest and best of young Frenchmen in the third decade of the nineteenth century, was at once a religion and a philosophy of life. Saint-Simon, the noble but eccentric genius who was the founder of the movement, set himself in opposition to the destructive spirit of the French Revolution, and advocated a reconstruction of society on the lines of what afterwards came to

88

be called socialism. He thought that the time had
come for the supersession of the feudal and military
system by an industrial order controlled by industrial
chiefs, and wished to see the spiritual direction of the
community pass from churchmen to men of science.
In his *Nouveau Christianisme*, published in 1825,
the year of his death, he made the precept ' Love one
another ' the basis of the new society he sought to
establish, and interpreted it as meaning that the
primary aim of social life should be the amelioration
of the physical, intellectual, and moral lot of the
poorest and most numerous class. After his death
his doctrines underwent an extraordinary transformation, and revealed an unexpected power to
provoke men to new thoughts and new actions. In
place of the crude philosophy of Saint-Simon, hark-
ing back to the physiological psychologists of the
previous century, the two leaders of the movement,
Enfantin and Bazard, created a system of thought in
which the sensationalism of the master was curiously
blended with mysticism. They found in the doctrine
of the divine trinity the key to the nature of man
and of the world. " Man," says Enfantin, "is God,
not in the infinite order, but in the indefinite order
of mind and the finite order of body. In these two
abstract worlds, he is the *will* of God. Of himself,
he loves, he thinks, he acts. . . . Let science then
seek to know the threefold life of man : the life of
activity, as though it were absolutely independent

of the non-ego ; his impersonal and passive life, as if it were absolutely dependent on the non-ego ; and finally his life of relation, the religious life, the life of union, of the marriage of the ego and the non-ego, a perpetual exchange of activity and passivity, of liberty and obedience, of loving and being loved." [1] But Saint-Simonism was far more than a mere system of doctrine. It was also a social evangel. It impelled its disciples to give creative effect to their ideals of life, and provoked a zeal for the regeneration of humanity which found practical outlet in a great variety of social experiments.

This was the movement which laid its spell on Seguin in the formative years of his life, and the influence of it continued with him to the end, long after the movement itself had passed into the limbo of lost causes and had been forgotten by the rest of the world. He accepted its metaphysic and its socialism, and made them the rule of his life. Inspired by the thought of the great potentialities of human nature even in its basest and most degraded forms, and filled with a great love for his poorer fellows, he dreamed of an education for the common people far wiser than the ordinary bookish education, an education like that which Rousseau planned for Emile, but within the reach of everybody. Especially he desired to make possible the education of

[1] *Science de l' Homme* (*Physiologie religieuse*), p. 50.

the idiot children with whose sad case he had become acquainted in the course of his medical studies. The general opinion was wholly against the possibility of lightening the idiot's darkened understanding. The great alienist Esquirol, under whose instruction he put himself in pursuance of his plans for idiot education, expressly declared that such an education was useless. "Idiots," he said, "are what they must remain for the rest of their life. Everything in them betrays an organization imperfect or arrested in its development. . . . No means are known by which a larger amount of reason or intelligence can be bestowed upon the unhappy idiot, even for the briefest period." [1] Seguin, regarding the idiot with the faith of a Saint-Simonian Christian, dared to believe that the mind could be set free from the bondage of its imperfect organs by a physiological education, and at the age of twenty-five he made his first attempt to educate an idiot boy. The result, attested by the generous witness of Esquirol, was marvellous. After eighteen months' training his pupil was able to make good use of his senses, could remember and compare, speak, write, and count. Encouraged by this success, he instituted

---

[1] The standard *Dictionnaire de Médicine*, published in 1837, the year in which Seguin began the educational treatment of idiocy, contains a statement to the same effect: "It is useless to combat idiocy. In order to establish intellectual activity, it would be necessary to change the conformation of organs which are beyond the reach of all modification."

a school for idiots, and continued the work thus happily begun on a larger scale. Five years later a commission of the Parisian Academy of Sciences, appointed at his request to examine ten of his pupils, reported that he had undoubtedly solved the problem of idiot education. All this while he had been issuing pamphlets and books explaining his methods, and in 1846 he published an epoch-making work on *The Moral Treatment, Hygiene, and Education of Idiots and other Backward Children*. The book won immediate recognition. It was crowned by the Academy, and its author received an autograph letter from Pope Pius IX thanking him for the services he had rendered to humanity. What was perhaps most gratifying to Seguin, it attracted the attention of all interested in the treatment of mental defects. Alienists of all nations came to Paris to see the work done by Seguin and those whom he had instructed,[1] and institutions on the model of his schools began to spring up throughout the civilized world. But in the very hour of success came the Revolution of 1848, and Seguin's work in France was brought to an end. Distrusting the new regime of the Prince-President, he resolved to become a citizen of the great Republic

[1] *Chambers's Journal* for 1847 has three articles by Mr Cleaton, the superintendent of an English asylum, giving an interesting account of a visit to the Bicêtre, and describing in detail the methods and results of the system of idiot-training employed there.

across the Atlantic. For a time he was in general practice in Ohio, and subsequently presided over the Pennsylvania Training School for Idiots. But he was hampered by his lack of facility in the use of English, and he found the details of institutional supervision rather irksome. Consequently, after a visit to France, he withdrew from this work and settled down in New York, and there spent the last twenty years of his life. His interest in the organization of institutions for the educational treatment of idiots remained unabated, and he willingly gave his help and advice to those concerned with them. The invention of the clinical thermometer and the investigation of animal heat, begun by him during these years and afterwards continued by his son, showed that he was more than a teacher of idiots. It was appropriate that the last enterprise of his life should be the establishment of a Physiological School for Weak-Minded and Weak-Bodied Children in the city of New York. "The application of physiology to education," he said in the prospectus of this school, "was the work of my youth and has been the main object of my thoughts for forty-two years. I give it my last years." But within a week or two of writing these words death came. The task of his life, however, had been accomplished years before. He had lived to see the desire of his youth abundantly realized and his principles and methods made the basis of idiot education all over the world.

From Locke to Montessori

For Seguin the education of idiots is not a thing apart. Its end is the same as that of ordinary education, and its methods ought to be simply adaptations of ordinary methods to the special case of the mentally deficient. That is not to say that the instruction commonly given to children in the schools is suitable for idiots. It is not even suitable, in Seguin's opinion, for normal children. In the people's schools thousands of pupils are herded together as in so many barracks without the least thought being given to their diverse physical aptitudes, or their varied physiological needs, or their different mental dispositions; and day by day four or five rations of intellectual provender are served out to them indiscriminately. Memory is the one faculty called into play : all the other faculties of body and soul are neglected, and their organs allowed to become atrophied and useless. What is wanted in place of this education that degrades all to the same dead level of unintelligent equality is an education that will embrace every mode of individual vitality, an education for the whole man, in every faculty, function, and aptitude. " Respect of individuality," Seguin declares in a notable passage, "is the first test of a teacher. At first sight all children look much alike ; at the second their countless differences appear like

94

countless obstacles; but better viewed, these differences resolve themselves into groups easily understood and not unmanageable. We find congenital or acquired anomalies of functions which need to be suppressed or to be given a better employment; deficiencies to be supplied; peculiarities to be watched; eccentricities to be guarded against; propensities needing a genial object; mental aptness or organic fitness requiring specific openings. This much at least, and more if possible, will secure the sanctity of true originality against the violent sameness of that most considerable part of education, the general training." [1]

The essential problem of education, according to Seguin, is this: "Given an individual or a people (it matters not which), to develop all that pertains to him or it in such fashion that the functions acquire their maximum activity, speed, extent, and precision—cerebral functions, muscular functions, sensorial functions, organs of thought, of movement, and of sensation." [2] In the case of ordinary children this problem though multiple in its terms is simple in its solution. All that is needed is to regularize the use of healthy organs and to extend the sphere in which their functions act freely and easily. In the case of idiots there is a further problem in the existence of a pathological condition of the nervous

[1] *Idiocy*, p. 33.

[2] *Traitement moral, Hygiène, et Education des Idiots*, p. 342.

system which is often difficult to diagnose and to treat. Here it is not a question of organs waiting for exercise to develop their powers. By one means or another the different modes of vitality have to be roused from their torpor and made fit to do their work before education can begin.

But whether the educator is dealing with ordinary children or with idiots, the fundamental principles of his methods are constant. Both groups share a common nature, and the problems they present, though of different difficulty, are ultimately the same. Man is a living trinity who is conscious of himself as both a unit and a threefold being in all his vital manifestations. He feels, understands, and wills at every moment of his existence, and can only attain his complete development if all the resources of pedagogy are employed to impart to him the maximum of sensibility, intellect, and morality. But though the whole man is present in every phase, education does not deal with all three aspects of his nature at once. Revelation and experience unite in showing that in the order of growth man moves and feels before he knows, and knows for a long time before he has consciousness of the moral significance of his acts and ideas. For this reason, education must deal with the activity of body before the mental functions and with the mental functions before the will. This serial order may seem to be inconsistent with the unity of human nature, but it is not really so. The distinction of elements is exaggerated by language, which gives to the results of an abstract analysis an apparent but misleading independence. Though in the first stage of education it is the body and its activities which are the main concern, the whole personality is at school. The teacher cannot train the child to move and feel rightly without acting at the same time on his intellect and calling forth his will. " It is impossible to take hold of the muscular apparatus without acting on the nerves, bones, etc., as it is equally impossible to command these special instruments of activity without exercising besides a reflex action on the intellect and the will." [1] So again at the second stage, when intellect is the central interest, the relation of mind to conduct is bound to be taken into account if mind itself is to be developed as it should. The difference of stages is a difference within the unity of life ; and so long as we remember the interdependence of functions, the idea of a sequence in development from the physical to the moral, though of less significance than Comte makes it, is of great value as a guide in educational practice. It leads the educator to pay his first attentions to the organic functions. Until the automatic movements are in large measure corrected and the graver deficiencies of the muscular apparatus made good, it is vain to think of beginning the proper

[1] *Idiocy*, p. 98.

work of education. "How could we expect," Seguin asks, "to ripen a crop of intellectual faculties on a field obstructed by disordered functions?"[1] Nurse and doctor must play their part in the preparation for education, by making the necessary hygienic and medical provision for the establishment and maintenance of bodily health.

Then comes the education of the body, or, rather, the education of activity, as Seguin prefers to designate it, in order to indicate that it is a psychical as well as a physiological process. This has to be considered in its two correlative aspects —motility and sensibility. Motility, the capacity for movement, includes a great number of the acts, functions, habits, and gestures by means of which the individual gets into relation with the world around him and gives outward expression to his inner impulses. Sensibility, the capacity for sense-perceptions, having as its media the various organs of sense distributed over the surface of the body, brings to the sensorium the notion of the external agents which have modified them and gives the outward facts inner form. The ordinary education is so much preoccupied with mind that it forgets the body altogether and leaves the training of motility and sensibility to chance. But on the unitary view of human nature that is plainly wrong. Body needs training quite as much as mind, to play

[1] *Idiocy*, p. 95.

its part in a complete life. Even in the best endowed children the movements of the body are never so regular and efficient as most people imagine, and in idiots almost all of them exhibit anomalies or incapacities of some kind or other. It is the same with the senses. In normal and still more in abnormal cases they also stand in need of a long course of special treatment, to make their functions more regular, more precise, and more expeditious.

MOTOR EDUCATION

Though there is such endless diversity in the malformations and defects due to idiocy that education in every instance requires to be largely individual, there are certain broad features common to all cases. There is on the one hand in most idiots a partial loss of the power of movement, shown by the child remaining fixed as he is placed or by his inability to take hold of anything, even to carry food to his mouth; and, on the other hand, there are all kinds of disordered movements, for the most part localized in the wrists and fingers, which tend to thwart all efforts to stimulate the immobile organs to their proper activity. The general principle of treatment is not to concentrate attention on any single defect, but to deal with it as part of the more general impotence of motor function. The first necessity is to change the negative immobility of idiocy into the deliberate immobility which is the starting-point in all normal action. The child must learn to stand, sit, recline, etc., of his own will before any progress is possible. As soon as he gains even partial command over his movements and can remain at rest to some extent, training in walking is made to alternate with the maintenance of a fixed position. If he is so inert that he cannot or will not move, the teacher brings about the essential motions, employing for that purpose instruments of passive exercise which as far as possible produce activity in the same way as personal impulses. If the legs do not bend, they are made to yield by means of a baby-jumper. If the feet do not come forward in the walking actions, they are brought into contact with a spring-board with the regularity of a walk. If the child still refuses to walk on the level ground after this passive training, he is set up on two blocks of wood of the same size as his feet, and he finds that he can only avoid a fall by standing up. In this situation " he must strain his muscles in readiness for any emergency. . . . He does not know exactly what to do nor what not to do ; but his strength is gathered, and if we have in front of him other steps and if we help him a little at first . . . he will try in the prospect of escaping the isolation to pass one foot on the next step, on another and on another, anxious, crying, but walking in fact for the first time." He now learns to use his hands for the maintenance of his balance, but even then his movements of progression show the peculiar lateral swaying so characteristic of idiots. To cure this two kinds of exercise are necessary. The first are exercises acting on the limbs separately : walking up various grades of stairs and stepping between the rounds of a ladder on the ground, for the training of the legs ; practice with dumb-bells, clubs, and arm extensions, for the training of the arms. The second consists of walking practice in a confined space, where the condition and slope of the ground calls for co-ordinated actions of the arms and legs. Once he can walk without swaying he is set to tread on a series of footprints which wind about in unexpected directions. "The act of directing each foot on each form is one of the best exercises for limbs which have previously escaped all control ; but what a superior exercise it is for the head above which has never suspected its regulating power. To walk among so many difficulties is to think." To give him practice in his newly acquired art, the child is now made to join a company of children who are busy performing the same movements on a large scale with the stimulus of example and of music. The result is marvellous. The previous tears are dried, tumbles are laughed at, torpor disappears. The first rays of promise have pierced through the darkness of idiocy.

After steadiness of foot has been acquired and the

body has at last got a firm base, it is time for the training of hand to begin. The first aim here is to develop the power of prehension and make the child able to grasp, to hold, and to let go. If he cannot or will not use his hands, he is put in front of an inclined ladder, with his feet on one round and his hands on another. He must grasp or fall. Generally he falls. In that case the teacher who has kept hold of him and not allowed him to get hurt replaces him on the ladder and lets him go on falling until he realizes that he can only save himself by grasping. If this plan does not succeed, he is set on a perpendicular ladder, and his hands are kept on the rounds by the teacher until they come to acquire power. Then he is put behind the inclined ladder with his hands on one of the top rounds, his feet are kicked away, and he lowers himself from round to round, partly by his own grasp and partly with the aid of the teacher. But if this exercise is not to do more harm than good, the frightened grasp must be instantly made to seize and carry things for a less instinctive use. It is a fundamental principle, applicable to all education, that as soon as a function begins to be accomplished mechanically it should at once be turned to account for more and more intellectual purposes, with no halt in the movement of progress, till the function is elevated to the rank of a capacity. Otherwise it will never enter into the higher life of the soul, and development will be arrested. Suppose in the present case that the boy after coming down from the ladder is looking at his slightly bruised hands. If he is left with the impression of injury he will certainly offer more resistance at the next trial. To prevent that an apple is put into each hand. Partly to feel the coolness on the burning surfaces, partly to keep the apple from falling, he contracts the fingers and gets a circular, equable, willed prehension. The mechanical act of grasping has got a new meaning and value.

The inclined ladder, though a useful piece of apparatus, must not be employed too long or too exclusively. If used to excess it elevates or rounds the shoulders, stiffens the joints, and unfits the hand for light and quick work. To increase the prehensile power, therefore, exercises involving more rapid action should go on concurrently with it. On the principle of contrast, which is fundamental in all education, the child ought to pass from a heavy prehension to a light one, and from a long one to a short one. Hand-training on these lines goes on for years, not so much with special apparatus as with articles in daily use ; and in course of time the formal prehension which is mainly physical in character develops into handling which is more specialized and therefore more intellectual. Then it is time to set the idiot to work, not merely for the physical or the intellectual advantages (though these are considerable), but for the moral effects. The obstacles to be encountered are great. The child's hands are still weak and clumsy ; his movements have no regularity or steadiness ; his mind has no conception of the worth of what is done and no persistence of purpose. Even when he gets past this stage his resolution is easily exhausted, and it is not uncommon to see the forehead or the hand covered with great drops of perspiration at the beginning of a thought or an action. Yet the lightest and easiest work done steadily, by imitation or by repetition, is better than nothing. The girl who begins to wipe the dishes, the boy who picks stones in the fields, are helping to save themselves from the horrors of idiocy. They have begun to acquire the aggressive power of the hand over foreign bodies which enables man to transform matter into the likeness of some ideal, and develops in him all the highest qualities of mind and character.

For the most part the gymnastic apparatus employed in this first training is of the simplest kind. While making occasional use of instruments like the ladders, Seguin attached greater importance to exercises borrowed from the daily life and occupations of ordinary children. He regarded the spade, the wheelbarrow, the watering-pot, the bow, the wooden horse, the hammer, and the ball as superior for most purposes to the more formal apparatus. At the same time he found it necessary to invent various instruments for the treatment of special deficiencies of organs and functions, and a brief account of the chief of these will serve to indicate how the work begun by disciplining the foot and the hand was extended to the body as a whole. One of the most valuable pieces of apparatus is the back-board, used for straightening out all kinds of bodily deformities. The board is ten inches wide, long enough to stand against a wall like a ladder, and fitted with rounds projecting laterally in pairs, ten inches apart. The child lies on his back on the board, raises his arms to seize two rounds, and puts his feet on the pair nearest the ground. Step by step he pulls himself up to the top round; then after a rest he descends in the same slow fashion, partly by his own efforts, partly with the help of his teacher. As a result of exercises of this type, differences between the shoulders, curvature of the spine, shortness of one limb, and similar irregularities slowly but surely disappear. Another valuable piece of apparatus is a special swing, which acts against a spring-board and is capable of being kept in motion by the child himself. Unlike the ordinary swing, which tends to depress the nervous system and to produce indolence, this swing stimulates the motor powers of the child, strengthening the arms, legs, neck, and spine, or overcoming the hypersensibility of the hand or foot, according to the special needs of the case. Dumb-bells are also serviceable for many purposes. Used physiologically and not merely to give a momentum to automatic balancing, they regulate general equilibrium, make irregular movements regular, teach how to grasp and to let go, impress obedience to commands on the part of both sides of the body or of only one. So employed, they act on the mind as much as on the body. One of the instruments of most general utility is the balancing-pole, which is a wooden stick about four feet long, with wooden balls at both ends. To strengthen the fingers it is thrown back and forward between teacher and child, with progressive force and rapidity from increasing distances. But delicacy of prehension is even more important than strength, and calls for a great number and variety of exercises complementary to the strengthening exercises. Nails are put into holes in a board which they exactly fit and then taken out again; geometrical figures are inserted into the spaces corresponding to them; pins, coins, and other minute articles are picked up from a smooth table; beads are threaded; clothes are buttoned and unbuttoned, laced and unlaced, etc. By means of such exercises and many more of the same kind, the child's fingers become adapted to every possible form of hand action and prepared for aggressive work on matter.

Up to this point the child has been learning to act and walk, either by a passive process with somebody or something impelling him, or half actively at the command of the teacher. He is now ready for an advance in the direction of personal activity. It is the capacity for imitation which makes this new progress possible. Imitation, which is as natural to idiots as to other human beings, is neither entirely passive nor entirely active. Its initiation is passive, its performance is active. Its modes are prescribed, its execution is voluntary. Hence its remedial power at this stage.

Imitation takes two forms. When it is some bodily action like the lifting of the arm which is imitated, it may be described as personal imitation. When it is an action affecting some external thing, as, for example, when the teacher sets a book upright on the table and the child does the same, it may be described as objective imitation. Both are of great importance, and especially the personal form. Never too soon commenced, never too much practised, personal imitation creates precision and rapidity, as gymnastics have created strength and endurance. First of all, movements of the whole body (such as sitting, standing, kneeling, etc.) are learned by imitation. Then follow movements of particular organs—the eyelids, the lips, the tongue, the fingers, and so forth. But the exercises are never allowed to become stereotyped even when special anomalies are being dealt with. The child is required to be ready for the sudden, unexpected call into action of any organ which can be moved by the will. The effect is soon apparent in the increasing intelligence of his countenance.

Until the pupil attains some degree of facility the imitation lesson is conducted individually. But as soon as possible advantage is taken of the contagious power of group imitation. Children at the same stage of advancement are brought together. If the lesson is new they are arranged so that it is mainly the teacher whom they see. If the lesson is familiar and the chief object is to get a more correct and a more rapid performance of it, they are arranged so that they can see each other as well as the teacher, and thus get the benefit of a double stimulus. Here is a typical lesson recorded by Seguin : " The first attitude is upright immobility. Without saying a word, we dictate with gestures the following attitudes : feet closed, feet open : forward the left foot, feet again closed. Raise the right knee, raise the left : a firm slap of the left hand upon it, and motionless. . . . Next we dictate more special positions. Face right, face left, hands raised, one foot forward, left hand out, both hands out, close the fists, open them, shut them again. Extend the index fingers, bring them together, shut them . . . and many more combinations easier to find than to describe, closing with three cheers and three claps of the hands. . . . Final immobility." [1]

[1] *Idiocy*, p. 130.

Exercises like these, done by imitation without a word passing between teacher and scholars, are invaluable. They quicken the movements, improve the function of sight, extend the range of the perceptions, give accuracy to the understanding, bring the whole body under the control of the will, and, above all, educate the dead hand for living work.

It is a long, slow business. But after months of alternate individual and group training, in fatigue, often in despondency, the teacher has the satisfaction of seeing his pupils not only imitating the physiological exercises, but carrying their new-found powers of imitation into the habits of daily life. He sees them trying to eat, dress, and stand as he himself does, proffering their services to weaker children as he did to them, and finally doing under the influence of habit what more gifted children only do under compulsion.

SENSORY EDUCATION

Once the anomalies of the muscular system have been corrected, those of the senses present themselves as the most serious impediment to further progress; and the training of the senses, which up to this point has been merely incidental, now becomes systematic and sustained. In this training the fundamental principle of psycho-physiological education must be kept definitely in mind—viz.

that each function of the life of relation is virtually, and must be made effectively, identical with its faculty. Under the artificial training of schools and colleges the sensorial and the intellectual development of children appear quite disconnected and even antagonistic, the exclusive training of the function impairing the faculty, the exclusive training of the faculty causing the function to become atrophied. In a true education the exercise of each function should give rise to a corresponding exercise of the related faculty. In the case of the senses each sense must be taught as a function, and taught besides as a faculty.

The sense of touch being that out of which all the others have developed, and the earliest in functional activity, is the first to get attention. As a rule the tactile sense of the idiot hand is very obtuse, but after a course of exercises in prehension it is generally ready for training. The cause of its defects must be first ascertained. It may be mainly the imperfection of the peripheral nerve-endings which are the seat of touch, or of the sensorial ganglia which are the seat of feeling, or of the nerves connecting these two. It may even be a general lack of comprehension due to a morbid condition of the cerebral hemispheres. Omitting consideration of the last of these, seeing that it is not peculiar to any one sense, it is evident that a threefold training is indicated : one to improve the act of perception, one to aid the transmission from nerve-ending to ganglia, one to enable the ganglia to convert impressions into knowledge. All three need to be given to some extent in every instance, but the special features of the case will determine which part of the function requires training most. Sometimes the peripheral termini of the nerves of touch are too sensitive. The skin must then be thickened by handling bricks, digging with a spade, sawing, etc., at the same time as the phalanges are being made more supple by means of passive exercises. At other times the hands are dull and insensible, and quite different treatment is called for. The child must handle objects which are substantial but not rough, and feel bodies of various degrees of polish or resistance. He must also plunge his hands alternately into cold and hot liquids, and learn to recognize by touch bodies of different softness or elasticity, such as eider-down, shells, flour, small shot, etc. If it is the centripetal nerves which are at fault, the exercise of throwing the balancing-pole will generally prove efficacious. But if after all this treatment the defect still remains, there is reason to suspect that it is either in the sensorial ganglia or in the cerebral hemispheres. In that case the hand exercises are continued daily, and hygiene and medicine are called in to supplement them by producing a general constitutional improvement.

About taste and smell, the senses most nearly

akin to touch, not much needs to be said. But it would be a mistake to neglect them altogether, because the normal use of food and perfumes has both an immediate and a lasting effect on idiots. The immediate effect is to make them sensitive with regard to what is dirty and to what is pleasant, and desirous of avoiding the one and enjoying the other. With proper care this makes it possible to exercise the mind of the child on sensorial tastes and distastes, and gives opportunities for comparisons and judgments on matters pertaining to personal feeling. The more permanent effect appears in the general tendency of children who have been educated in the enjoyment of cleanliness, good food, and fresh air to aspire to worthy conditions of existence and to shrink from the life of the streets and of beggary which is the common lot of uneducated idiots.

Imperfections of hearing and speech have the same varied causation as those of touch. The cases of prime interest here are those of intellectual deafness due to idiocy. The ear which does not hear, not because of any organic defect but by reason of some central failure, needs to be exercised in the hearing of noises, music, and speech. Noises are connected with wants, music with the motive powers, speech with the intellect.

The sounds of noises may be called the hieroglyphics of phenomena. They *mean* the things that produce the phenomena : one means pouring rain, another means the rushing of the winds, another means the frying in the pan which awakens the child's appetite. The wild boy educated by Itard did not hear the report of a pistol discharged behind his head, but heard the fall of a nut on the floor. If water is poured from one vessel into another near an apparently deaf idiot when he is thirsty, he will turn his head and go for a drink. From this it is evident that significant noises may help to arouse attention and to make the ear quick and responsive.

Music has more varied and lasting applications than noises in the treatment of deaf idiots. Even when it has no special meaning for them, it is capable of exciting impulses before unknown and producing profound emotional effects. It gives rest from hard labour. It causes in the immobile child a tremulousness of all the fibres which is easily converted into incipiency of action. It awakens and quickens thought. It dissipates anger, weariness, and melancholy, and disposes to gentle feelings. It is an unrivalled moral sedative. Hence music ought to enter largely into the daily life of an institution for the education of idiot children. Under these conditions, the child who does not care for music, or who does not hear it, will gradually get his sensibility aroused. When tunes are being played he should be allowed to place his hands, or even his chest, against the piano ; and the player should play loudly, then softly, and occasionally stop altogether, so that the contrasts may induce an appreciation of musical sounds. Alternately with this group lesson, the child should sometimes be kept in solitude, even in darkness, and hear the sounds of distant music undistracted by the noise and movement of other children. Sooner or later the strains will make their way into the dull ears. Once there is evidence of sensibility the attempt can be made to transform the simple function of hearing into the capacity for listening, by breaking the continuity of the tune at its most interesting accent-point, and leaving the child's ear on the alert, eager for more.

From music there is a natural transition to speech. The rudiments of speech are already present in the instinctive language of cries and screams. By the imitation of musical notes, these animal cries are easily changed into vowel sounds. At the same time exercises of imitation are recommenced morning and evening to teach the child to articulate the various consonants. All the parts of the face are moved in correlation with the fingers, and mimicry is invoked with the double object of giving him an analytical survey of the different parts involved in the act of speech, by touch, sight, and movement, and of leading him to execute the necessary actions after the teacher. Then the vowels and the consonants are brought together in suitable combination. The first difficulties are overcome with the help of music, and this is followed up by imitative practice in the emission of simple, double, and compound syllables, with or without music, with or without formal commands. There is still a long interval, however, between this mechanical speech and true language, and probably the child will go on for a time uttering his own uncouth sounds as if he had learned nothing from the arduous teaching of syllables and words. Whatever happens, the teacher must on no account interfere with the spontaneity of his utterances. No good purpose is served by attempting to force speech on him prematurely. The chances are that what the child learns will not appear at once, but will reveal itself at a later time. Or what he learned and did not show in private will appear when he takes his place in the group. Or what neither private nor group training brings out may flow from his lips without effort on some chance occasion. We sow, and nature fecundates.

The last sense to receive special training is sight. As sight is the most intellectual of all the senses and the one whose anomalies are the most varied and the most closely connected with intellectual disorders in idiocy, its culture is correspondingly important. The first thing necessary is to give it fixity. There are many exercises of value for this purpose. The child, for example, may be set to find with the eye things in daily use which he has been accustomed to get by touch. Or he may be put in a dark room and shown geometrical and other figures outlined in light. The wonderful combinations of colours produced in the kaleidoscope have also an extraordinary attraction, and the exercises with the balancing-pole are quite as effective in steadying the eye as in training the hand. But the best means of all is the steady look of the teacher. He gets the child in front of him, away from all distracting noise, in such a position that the whole body can be kept perfectly immobile, and looks into his eyes with an intense and persevering stare. The child tries to avoid his look, throws himself about, screams, and shuts his eyes. The teacher waits calmly, and as soon as the eyes open again he repeats the look. This may go on for days, or weeks, or even months, but generally success comes in the end, and the child has gained a new power. Instead of using touch or smell to give him knowledge of phenomena, he uses sight, at first concurrently with the other senses, and after a while almost exclusively. In the more refractory cases the direct individual exercises of the look need to be alternated with the sight of groups of children at work. Their various activities attract and ultimately hold the wandering attention.

When the eye has become steady even to the smallest extent the child is made acquainted with those properties of bodies which are perceived by sight, notably colour, shape, size, distance, and arrangement.

Edouard Seguin

(*a*) Colours are taught in the dark room with coloured window-panes, or with things like cards, ribbons, and marbles, which are of different or similar colours and capable of being arranged in pairs. Coloured balls and cups of the same colour into which they may be put, and other contrivances of a like kind for pairing colours, may also be used. The familiarity acquired with colours in these ways should then find application with respect to articles of daily use or enjoyment.

(*b*) The appreciation of the shape of things has its basis in the knowledge of a few typical forms, of which the simplest are circles, squares, and triangles. These should be taught to the child both as types and in their concrete embodiment in common objects, attention being specially directed to the contrasts involved. Blocks shaped like dominoes are of great value in showing the combination of forms produced by the juxtaposition or superposition of objects. In this lesson, which is taught by the method of objective imitation, child and teacher sit on opposite sides of a table, each with a small pile of blocks. The teacher puts a block in various positions; the child follows his example. The same thing is done with two, three, four, or more blocks, till the exercise of simple imitation becomes quite intellectual, and requires careful attention and considerable power of combination. To relieve the tension which is unavoidable in these exercises, the lesson ends with the building of walls, towers, and other fabrics on a large scale.

(c) The dimensions of bodies are appreciated by measurement, which is effected by the sight, by the hand, or by special instruments. In the case of idiots a beginning is made with measurement by sight. In one lesson, for example, ten sticks measuring one decimetre, two decimetres, and so on in sequence up to a metre, are used. After comparison of the longest and the shortest, they are all mixed up, and the child is called on to arrange them serially, beginning with the longest or the shortest. The skill acquired in performing this task is sometimes far greater than that possessed by the ordinary adult. The notion of distance also needs to be imparted by means of simple preliminary exercises. The teacher places things of the same kind (for example, books) at different distances from each other, and makes the child do the same, at first by imitation and afterwards by command. When distances are to be measured in a room, from point to point, or from person to person or thing, the child is led to think of himself as at the centre of a circle, at equal distances from certain points, at greater or less distances from others. The same comparative method is adopted with more remote objects in the open air.

When the fundamental attributes of the objects of vision are realized in these elementary ways, the

Edouard Seguin

time has come to make a beginning with drawing
and the other arts by which matter is idealized.
Often, however, the idiot child has no proper understanding of what a plane surface is ; and as this
knowledge is essential not merely for drawing but
for a great many actions in ordinary life, it is necessary to take some pains to teach it to him. He is
set to make a level or a rounded surface on sand,
with his hand or a spade or a roller. The plane for
writing or drawing is studied by the teacher marking
the centre, the corners, and other points on a circum-
scribed surface with wafers, and getting the child to
do the same on another. The idea of the plane is
got even better by touching with the fingers every
prominent point of a limited surface like a slate.
When the child begins to show competence in these
exercises, the teacher takes a pencil in his own hand
and puts one in his pupil's hand. He then draws
a line slowly and distinctly from the top of the slate
to the bottom, and the child tries to do the same.
In some cases the result is almost total failure.
The child has acquired the virtual capacity to draw
lines, as he shows by his movements, but lacks the
nervous power to do so. The attempt produces
unmistakable signs of fatigue, even on the part of
some who are capable of lifting heavy weights or
of doing a whole day's work in the fields. Before
further progress is possible the nerves of the
hand need to be strengthened by preparatory

exercises. This happily is effected by some of the arts akin to drawing which employ other instruments than the pen or the pencil. The child, for example, may be given some plastic material like clay or putty to shape into squares, rounds, or triangles, or to make into the form of familiar objects. Or he may be given a piece of soft wood to be whittled with a knife to certain marks so as to produce some well-known shape. Soon the teacher dispenses with the marks and only gives a pattern to be copied ; and finally gets him to work without any pattern at all. Similar work is done afterwards with the chisel, the hatchet, and the saw. Another useful occupation is rag- or paper-cutting with scissors. The child gets patterns of card or wood and has to cut out similar forms from rags or newspapers. At first the paper is placed directly on the pattern. After a time the pattern to be copied is put in front of the child. Then when skill has increased the pattern is merely shown and put out of sight. Finally no pattern is shown at all and the child is compelled to work entirely from memory.

This representation of things in the solid (or, as Seguin calls it, 'substantial drawing') has a double purpose to serve. In the first place, it gives the child the power of expressing simple ideas of form by the work of his hands—a power of the greatest value even for the normal child. In the second place, even when the intellectual result is very imperfectly attained, it gives the child the firmness and precision of hand which is necessary for drawing and writing.

A beginning is made in drawing by the familiar method of imitation. The teacher draws straight lines in various positions and relations on the qlackboard, and the pupil follows suit. Once the straight line can be drawn with tolerable accuracy the same plan is followed with curved lines. Then straight lines and curved lines are used in combination to produce an unlimited variety of figures, and out of this practice writing is gradually evolved. Contrary to school usage, but agreeably to nature (as Seguin thinks), the letters are written like the teacher's model before being read, and only receive names when they have become perfectly familiar.

This work, it should be noted, is not intended to be a direct introduction to reading. Its primary object is to give accuracy to the sight. As a matter of fact, the method of Jacotot is adopted in the reading lessons, and attention is directed, not to the letters, but to the whole word. The child is led to perceive that each word has a form, a name, and a meaning. Words like 'bread,' 'apple,' 'book,' are put in front of the pupil on cards, and the teacher names the word, connecting it at the same time with the actual object. The pupil is then tested in various ways to make sure that the three-fold connexion has been established in his mind, and only when it is certain that that has been accomplished does the teacher pass on to new words.

In the first instance all this work is done individually. Minds so limited in comprehension and so lacking in tenacity as those of idiots need the concentration which is only got through individual teaching, if they are to make any advance. But as soon as possible advantage is taken of the stimulus of group learning to confirm and secure the advance that has been made. The alternation of the individual and the group methods is an essential feature of Seguin's system.

INTELLECTUAL AND MORAL EDUCATION

With the lessons on reading and language the idiot's education enters on a new phase. Up to this point he has been occupied with the notions of the physical properties of things given by the senses —the notions, for example, of their form, their arrangement, their dimensions, their smell, their savour. Now that he has gathered together a considerable number of notions as the material of his thought, he is ready to go on to learn about the relations of objects and to exercise his intellect on the forming of ideas. To take a particular case of this transition from notion to idea : he had a *notion* of a key when he was able to distinguish it from other things; he forms an *idea* of it when he learns its relation to the lock. Here as always the idea of a concrete thing arises from the combination of two or more notions. It is their relation, their *raison d'être*, their purpose. The child's progress in reading and the learning of grammatical speech— processes which go on concurrently—is essentially an acquiring of ideas. A beginning is made with the simple identification and naming of common objects and experiences, such as form the gist of his first reading matter. But the notion or knowledge of the identity of things which is given with the name only satisfies his curiosity for a very short time. Even the lowest idiot is not content with the mere recognition of a round or a square. He touches and licks it when it is put before him, to discover whether it has any other qualities than shape. Consequently the teacher must soon pass beyond the elementary operation of naming, and introduce the pupil more or less systematically to the essential properties of objects. The qualities perceived in the earlier gymnastic of the senses are the first to be noted, but they are studied no longer than is necessary to develop the analytical power of the child. As soon as the development of his intelligence permits, he should be led by means of object-lessons beyond the physical properties of objects to their moral and intellectual qualities and bearings. When this is not done the study of objects, instead of being a means of mental elevation, only serves to confine the mind in the region of the material. There is an infinite difference between the child who has only learned the constituent elements of a vegetable and one who has learned to grow it; or between one who has learned to produce it for the satisfaction of his own appetite and another who produces it for the support of children more destitute than himself.

One of the attributes of objects which requires the special attention of the educator is number. Most idiots cannot count beyond two, but when they are exercised with objects and qualities rather than with figures they gradually acquire a moderate power of numbering and computing, and some of them even manifest quite extraordinary mathematical ability.

All the while the child is becoming familiar with names, attributes, and numbers by this concrete discipline he should be getting trained in the use of those parts of speech which are required for the statement of relations. Attention should first be given to verbs, since these denote actions by means of which the connexions of men and of things are constantly being made and broken. If the child finds difficulty with the verb, the most effective way of making him comprehend its significance is to show him actions and the words denoting them in frequent association. Following on this, the more subtle relationship indicated by prepositions can be taught by a similar method. A simple study of pronouns and the other parts of speech completes this initial linguistic training, and the child is ready to enter into ordinary life and to receive the ordinary education.

But though intellectual education ends here so far as the teacher of idiots is concerned, his work is not yet complete. It still remains for him to turn the partially educated faculties of his pupils to practical account by preparing them to take their places as humble but useful members of society. For this there is needed a special training of memory and imagination, the two faculties which are of most importance in the conduct of life.

It is quite common to find memory restricted among the idiots to such capacities as musical imitation, counting, and mechanics. This one-sided memory is not of much use for the business of life until it has been transformed and broadened by exercises in the exact remembering of everyday facts. But these exercises should not be in any way formal. The mind must be habituated to remember not for the sake of remembering but with a view to practical needs. The earliest memory training has reference to the hygiene of the body, and includes the practice of cleanliness, proper ways of standing and walking, good habits of dressing and feeding. Subsequently the attempt has to be made to leave the child with strong memorial impressions of the value of time, money, food, fuel, clothing, light, home, labour, and of their bearings on his own life and the lives of others. Then when this class of commonplace and daily recollections has been brought to the working-point and is beginning to govern the habits of the child it is time, if the growing intelligence of the pupil permits, to pass from the physical to the moral, and implant in experience and memory the sense of kindness, of justice, and of beauty. The most urgent need of the idiot, however, is for the cultivation of those powers of body and mind which will enable him to do some useful work in the world. If his education stops short of this it must be written down as a failure. All that is abnormal in the social relations of the uneducated idiot is due to the fact that he makes no contribution to social well-being, but lives in a condition of helpless dependence. Train him to apply himself steadily to work of some kind, however lowly, and the intellectual and moral gain is enormous. The idiot becomes fit to regulate the present with reference to past and future, as every proper man must do.

To supplement the work of memory, imagination also needs training. Memory connects the past and future in the present of a single individual, and makes possible the organization of his life in its lowest as well as its highest concerns. Imagination goes further, and connects the individual with all mankind and with all time. Let imagination be cultivated, as memory was cultivated, in the simplest and most common affairs, and ultimately by a progressive education it may take the idiot child into the highest reaches of the human spirit. The sequence from the first stage to the last is unbroken. " From the feeling of pressure in the tactile organs which taught prehension to our feeling of duty toward our pupils which taught them affection, from the distinction of the difference between a circle and a square and that between right and wrong, we have followed a continuous path, beginning where the function awakes to the perception of simple notions, finishing where the faculties refuse to soar higher in the atmosphere of idealism." [1]

The successful issue of the task is a splendid vindication of the principles which guided and inspired it. " We looked at the rather unmovable or ungovernable mass called an idiot with the faith that where the appearance displayed nothing but ill-organized matter there was nothing but ill-circumstanced animus. In answer to that conviction, when we educated the muscles, contractility

[1] *Idiocy*, p. 199.

responded to our bidding with a spark of volition. We exercised severally the senses, but an impression could not be made upon their would-be material nature without the impression taking its rank among the accumulated idealities. We were enlarging the chest, and new voices came out of it, expressing new ideas and feelings. We strengthened the hand and it became the realizer of ideal creations and labour. We started imitation as a passive exercise and it soon gave rise to all sorts of spontaneous actions. We caused pleasure and pain to be felt through the skin, and the idiot in answer tried to please by the exhibition of his new moral qualities. In fact, we could not touch a fibre of his without receiving back the vibration of his all-souled instrument." [1]

Bibliographical Note

The external facts of Seguin's career are most adequately given in Appleton's *Cyclopædia of American Biography* (which gives a full list of his works) and in Hirsch's *Lexikon der Aerzte*. There is a more intimate account of some aspects of his life and work in a volume *In Memory of Edouard Seguin, M.D., being Remarks made by his Friends at the Lay Funeral Service held 31st October*, 1880 (New York), of which a good review appeared in *The British Journal of Mental Science* (1881). The most important of Seguin's own writings are his *Traitement moral, Hygiène, et Education des Idiots et des autres Enfants*

[1] *Idiocy*, p. 203.

Edouard Seguin

arrières (1846), and *Idiocy and its Treatment by the Physiological Method,* published in 1866 and reprinted in 1907 by Teachers' College, Columbia University. The three articles in *Chambers's Journal* (1847) already referred to give a good contemporary account of Seguin's system at work, and are specially valuable for the information they supply about the occupational training he designed for idiots.

CHAPTER VII

MARIA MONTESSORI

b. 1870

MARIA MONTESSORI was born during the closing years of the long struggle for Italian freedom and unity. The only child of parents not too well off, she grew to womanhood amid the rapidly changing conditions that followed on the setting up of the new Italy, and made personal acquaintance with some of the more pressing problems of modern life. She herself played a pioneer's part in the movement for the widening of woman's sphere which was one of the most notable features of the time. In defiance of prejudice, she entered the University of Rome as a medical student, and was the first woman in Italy to receive the degree of Doctor of Medicine. She began the practice of her profession, but a greater work was awaiting her. After graduation she was appointed assistant doctor at the psychiatric clinic of the university, and in the course of her duties she became interested in the feeble-minded children whom she found housed in the lunatic asylums she visited. She was led in this way to the study of the special methods of treatment devised for such cases by Seguin fifty years before. Following out his ideas, which had become obscured and forgotten with the lapse of time, she came to the conclusion that mental deficiency in children called for education even more than for medical treatment. Her advocacy of this view at an important educational congress in Turin in 1898 led to her being invited by the Minister of Education to deliver a course of lectures to the teachers of Rome on the observation and training of defective children. Out of this developed the Orthophrenic School—a school for the cure of feeble-minded children—which she conducted in person for two years, from 1898 to 1900. Not only did she train special teachers, but she herself took actual part in the teaching of the children from eight in the morning till seven in the evening; and, not content with her own experience, she visited London and Paris for the study of the best methods of educating the mentally defective.

All this time the conviction was growing in her mind that the methods she found successful in dealing with idiots were most of them quite applicable to normal children, and that the ordinary schools needed just such a transformation as she had effected in her own school. She was led to this view by her study of the works of the great Italian anthropologists, and especially of Giuseppe Sergi. Lombroso had devoted his genius to the investigation of the criminal, De Giovanni had carried anthropological methods into medicine. Sergi sought to turn anthropology from the study of abnormal persons to the discovery of means of preventing abnormality, by establishing a scientific pedagogy on the basis of an anthropology of childhood. "By means of education," says Dr Montessori, expressing his point of view and her own, "we shall seek to prevent the ultimate consequences of degeneration and disease. If criminal anthropology has been able to transform punishment in modern society, we ought to set ourselves *to transform the individual* in the school of the future. And with the triumph of this ideal, pedagogical anthropology will in large measure have taken the place of criminal anthropology, just as schools for the abnormal and the weak will in large measure have taken the place of jails and hospitals." [1]

What led her finally to turn her attention to the problems of ordinary education was the striking success of her work with the feeble-minded children. By special methods of her own contriving, she managed to teach a number of her pupils to read and write so well that they were able to be presented for examination at school on a level with ordinary children. Those who saw the results found them almost miraculous. For her part, the chief cause for wonder was that the normal pupils should do so badly. "While every one was admiring the progress

[1] *Antropologia Pedagogica*, p. 14.

of my idiots, I was searching for the reasons which could keep the happy, healthy children of the common schools on so low a plane that they could be equalled in tests of intelligence by my unfortunate pupils." Her own explanation was that while the idiot children had received an education which helped them in their psychic development, the others had been mentally depressed by the methods of the schools. With a view to helping in the regeneration of ordinary education, she gave up her work with the defectives and betook herself to further study. She returned to the university as a student of philosophy, devoted herself to experimental psychology as a propædeutic to the scientific pedagogy she hoped to have a part in establishing, and pursued her anthropological studies by various investigations among school children. At the same time she continued her study of the writings of Seguin. To make sure that she would get the spirit as well as the letter of his teaching, she translated into Italian his works on the educational treatment of idiocy, as well as the writings of his predecessor Itard.

In 1907 there came an opportunity to put her theories to the test of practice. The director of the Roman Association for Good Building, a philanthropic association concerned with the housing problem, conceived the idea of having a school attached to every tenement where all the little ones between the ages of three and seven could play and work under the supervision of a teacher living in the tenement, and he applied to Dr Montessori for her co-operation in carrying out the scheme. She agreed to direct the experiment on its educational side, and the first Children's House was opened in January of that year. It met with immediate success, and others soon followed. The methods evolved by Dr Montessori in the education of idiots were made the basis of the work. As time went on various modifications and additions which experience showed to be necessary were introduced, and the scheme took more or less final shape in the form presented in Dr Montessori's work, *The Method of Scientific Pedagogy applied to Infant Education in the Children's Houses* (given to the English public under the objectionable title of *The Montessori Method*).

The experiment is not yet concluded. Dr Montessori, indeed, has always maintained that it is only just beginning. If so, it is unfortunate that her own connexion with the Children's Houses was brought to an end in 1911, and that there is no longer any institution in which her method is at work under her personal direction. In spite of this partial breach in the continuity of her experiment, however, she is still busy, with the financial aid of the Montessori Society of the United Kingdom, extending her methods, and testing the possibility of applying them to the education of older children. The results of this experimentation still remain to be seen.

Educational Principles

Dr Montessori professes to be carrying on the tradition of Seguin in her educational work, but the differences between disciple and master are, to say the least, as deep as their agreements. Seguin lived in an age of great philosophical activity, and he shared the conviction of the majority of his contemporaries that it was impossible to comprehend the facts of the universe in a system of thought. His own metaphysic, indeed, was as the breath of life to him. It determined and inspired his life-work, and marked out the course he followed both in his personal conduct and in his science. Montessori, living a full half-century later in a time of philosophical disillusionment, shows in an exaggerated form the prevalent distrust of speculative thinking. She approaches educational questions, she imagines, without any of the philosophical ideas about the meaning and methods of education which in her opinion have vitiated the work of all previous educators and delayed the coming of a scientific pedagogy. It is her ideal to be a scientist pure and simple, an observer of the real facts of child development and nurture, unbiased by any preconceptions as to the nature and end of the process. As a matter of fact, neither the scientist nor the practical man ever does work without preconceptions. The simplest experiment presupposes some ideas about its objects and some anticipations about its outcome ; and these ideas and anticipations, with their implications, constitute a philosophy of some kind, which is likely to lead to confused thinking sooner or later if it is ignored. Even to disclaim a philosophy, as Montessori does, implies a philosophy. In her case the advocacy of an attitude of passivity in presence of the spontaneous manifestations of the child rests upon the vague doctrine (which has affinities with Nietzsche's thought) of a life-force expressing itself in the activities of body and of mind, and is connected with the idea (borrowed from Sergi) that for the educator as for the biologist the one reality is *the living individual*. Dr Montessori assuredly does not lack a philosophy of a kind.[1]

What she really means when she says that she approaches the study of pedagogy without preconceptions is that she is trying to see the educational facts in the light of experience and experiment, unobscured by the prejudices which dominate the ordinary education. In fact, it is not preconceptions she dispenses with : it is only fixed ideas which

[1] The introductory sections of her *Antropologia Pedagogica* throw a considerable light on Dr Montessori's philosophical premises. There, one is referred to Enrico Morselli as the source of her anti-speculative views (p. 17), and gets a brief statement of the doctrine of the living individual.

are not being constantly tested, and when necessary modified, by reference to fact. Her cult is not of the empty mind, but of the open mind.[1] This is at once the secret of her strength and of her weakness. Her criticism of many of the defects of the schools is undoubtedly effective. Much that she says about educational malpractices that go for the most part unquestioned, even if it has been said many times before, is at any rate worth saying again in the dialect of our own times, and she has said it convincingly. Most people whose minds have not been dulled by the accepted custom will agree with her about the cramping effects of the routine of home and school, and especially of group teaching, on the growing mind of the child. There is no doubt also that many of her practical suggestions are of great value. It would be strange if a woman of Dr Montessori's education and ability, with none of the idols of the tribe, had not been able to hit on some expedients of substantial worth for practical purposes. But criticism and teaching devices, however helpful in a casual way, are insufficient as a basis for such an educational reconstruction as she aspires to effect. For that there is necessary a more or less definite philosophy of life, such as is not provided by any method of observation and experiment. And here Dr Montessori fails. Unlike

[1] Her method may be described in the phrase of Mr Santayana as "following the lead of the subject-matter."

From Locke to Montessori

Pestalozzi, whose genius and work are recalled at times by hers, she has not succeeded in evolving a coherent and unified scheme of thought out of her experimentation. Her so-called method is not really one method, but an aggregation of methods, only loosely related in her own mind, and capable of being employed in detachment from each other without any serious loss of the virtue of any one of them.

The reason of this is not difficult to find. In her anxiety to let experience have free play and not to be hampered by uncriticised preconceptions, she has escaped the rigidity of the fixed idea only to fall into the opposite evil of eclecticism. Her own education, her own knowledge, her own experiments have become for her the measure of truth.[1] The guidance she does not get from a philosophy of life has come to her from the circumstances under which she has worked, and both in what it includes and in what it omits her educational programme has something of the haphazard character of its genesis. This is brought out very plainly by her own account of the development of her pedagogical ideas. Her educational work, as we have seen, began with the idiot children whom she found in the course of her professional duties in the asylums. She was led in this way to study the special method of training

[1] One is tempted to recall Lecky's remark about Spencer, that he "has an odd way of making his own knowledge and habits the measure of all sound education."

devised by Seguin for children such as these, and
though the principles underlying Seguin's apparatus
and exercises were as foreign to her own way of
thinking as those of any 'philosophical' educator,
she adopted the method as a working system and
applied it with great success. When she undertook
the education of normal children at a later time, she
made Seguin's devices (with certain modifications
in details) one of the main features of her scheme.
The discovery that <u>freedom is an essential require</u>-
ment of a true education, though in a way implicit
in her insistence on biological individuality, seems
only to have been made when she began to experiment with these children. In trying to educate
in accordance with the observed characters of her
pupils she saw that it was best both for her as
experimental educator and for the children with
whom she was dealing that there should be the
utmost possible liberty, and she set herself to devise
means of training which would fulfil this condition.
This introduced the second constituent into her
scheme. In working out her plan of a free education she made use of all kinds of occupations—the
tasks of daily life, plastic work, sensory exercises.
These last, which bulk most largely in her method,
belonged to Seguin's practice ; but the form they
took in her hands was due to her own studies in
experimental psychology. The tests for sensibility
were transformed by her into means for the

cultivation of sensibility. This psychological element in her system is so distinctive a feature of it as to be entitled its third constituent. Out of the sense-training, finally, there developed a preparation for later school life in the arts of reading, writing, and arithmetic. This was no part of her first intention, but the children whose senses had been trained stood in obvious need of some further occupation, and having no reason for excluding these subjects she yielded to the popular demand for their inclusion in the work of the Children's Houses. These may be regarded as the fourth constituent of her scheme.[1]

Amid the somewhat heterogeneous detail of the Montessori system two ideas stand out as more fundamental than the rest. The first is the need for freedom and spontaneity on the part of the developing child. The second is the importance of the training of the muscles and the senses in the first stages of education. By these the system stands or falls.

The doctrine of free development is perhaps the more central of the two. At any rate it is the one

---

[1] It is worthy of note that the elaborate system of anthropological measurements detailed in the *Antropologia Pedagogica*, which, according to Montessori and to her master Sergi, is the essential basis of a scientific pedagogy, does not seem to have influenced her educational practice in the slightest degree. The fact is that most of these measurements have only a very remote connexion with the work of education. The knowledge they give of individual characteristics is for the most part of no practical use; and even where it might conceivably be useful it is not used.

to which the English and American disciples of Dr Montessori attach the greater importance,[1] and our study of her methods will begin with it. What exactly is implied in the demand that the child should be free ? One's first inclination is to find in it an extension of the democratic view that freedom is the fundamental right of every human being, without respect to class, age, or sex, and to connect it with the long and varied struggle against exclusive privileges of every kind which has been going on since the French Revolution.[2] This is a view which has warrant in some of Montessori's own utterances. Nevertheless, though it contains an important element of truth, it would be a mistake to lay too much stress on it in the interpretation of her meaning ; for this kind of liberty, as Montessori says in claiming as against Rousseau to be the first to give the true concept of freedom to education, is only social liberty, which though an elevated idea is always partial and restricted.[3]

The primary meaning of freedom in Montessori's use of the term is the biological one. As a scientific student of the child, she insists on viewing him as

[1] The introduction which Mr E. G. A. Holmes contributes to Mrs Fisher's *A Montessori Mother* shows very plainly that it is this feature of the Montessori system which has won his support for it, and makes one suspect that his interest in sensory training, as practised by Montessori, is not very deep. It is the free spirit of the system rather than its particular contents which seems to appeal to him.

[2] *Cf.* Fisher, *A Montessori Mother*, ch. viii.

[3] *The Montessori Method*, p. 15.

she would view any other form of life, in his individual character as a unique expression of the
eternal life-force apart from all social modifications.
Her method, she says, "is established upon one
fundamental base—*the liberty of the pupils in their
spontaneous manifestations.*" [1] The child she regards as a being who grows in body and in soul by
reason of an inner impulse that has behind it the
great *élan vital* of the whole universe, and who only
needs to be left unrestricted to unfold his powers in
proper succession. From this point of view, the
essence of freedom is to be found in the absence of
anything which would mar or stifle the innate
powers. It is freedom to grow.

But Montessori does not stop, as some individual-
ists do, with the merely negative prescription of
non-interference. By identifying freedom with
independence, she contrives to give to the idea of
liberty what seems to be a positive content. "No
one," she contends, "can be free unless he is independent; therefore the first active manifestations
of the child's individual liberty must be so guided
that through this activity he may arrive at independence." [2] Here she has frankly given up the
biological idea of freedom, and is seeking to define
its character as a social attribute. The free man on
this view is one who is self-sufficient and does not

[1] *The Montessori Method*, p. 80.
[2] *Ibid.*, p. 95.

need the help of others in satisfying his essential needs. Dependence on others, in the case both of child and of man, implies limitation and the lack of freedom. " The paralytic who cannot take off his boots because of a pathological fact and the prince who dare not take them off because of a social fact are in reality reduced to the same condition." Neither of them is in any proper sense a free agent.

Now let us see what are the educational implications of Montessori's twofold conception of freedom. She begins, as we have noted, with the idea of life as essentially free activity. The growth of body and mind in obedience to the mysterious impulses of the life-force can only attain its full perfection if left unimpeded. " We cannot know the consequences of trifling a *spontaneous action* when the child is just beginning to be active : perhaps we stifle *life it-self.*" [1] For this reason the forced immobility and the forced learning of the schools are altogether wrong. Under the better conditions which Montessori aims at creating in the Children's Houses, the endeavour is made to give perfect liberty for development both on its physical and its mental sides. Fixed benches in which the children are cramped into an artificial quietness are replaced by movable furniture light enough to be handled by the children themselves, and complete freedom of movement is permitted. The same rule applies to learning.

[1] *The Montessori Method*, p. 87.

Each pupil does his own work and proceeds at his own pace. Except for special exercises, in which for the most part they can join or not as they please, there is no class instruction to compel them all to learn the same things in the same way. They learn when they wish and they stop when they wish. There is no teaching in the ordinary sense of the word. There is always a directress present, but she is primarily an observer and not a teacher. She sees that every child is busy in his own way, and provides him with the kind of work that her observation of him leads her to think is best suited for the stage of development he has reached. But she makes no attempt, direct or indirect, to compel him to do the work,[1] and she limits her guidance to what is required to set him on the path of self-education. If he fails to do a task which has been given him, she does not correct him or urge him to try it again. Failure means that he has not yet reached the stage of growth at which he is fit for the particular exercise, and there is nothing to be done but to wait, and to prepare him for it in the meantime by giving him some simpler exercise which will lead up to it. Any other method would involve the forcing

[1] Dr Montessori objects very strongly to rewards and punishments of every kind. She does not think that external inducements or external repressions have the least educative value. The only proper incentive to learning is the joy of the work. When that is present reward and punishment are equally unnecessary. When it is not present there is no education.

of the directress's personality on the child and the paralysing of his spontaneous activity.

This does not mean, however, that there is not to be an ordered progress in the development of the child's mind : only that the driving power is to come from within and not from without. This is secured by the special apparatus and exercises devised by Dr Montessori, which are such that as far as possible the child sees and corrects his own mistakes in using them. He is given a series of cubes, for example, and shown how to build them into a tower, with the largest at the base and the others becoming progressively smaller as they mount up. The cubes are then scattered, and the child is left to repeat the tower-building himself. If he makes the mistake of beginning with the second biggest instead of the biggest, he discovers his mistake when he is left with a cube for which he can find no place in the structure he has erected, and he generally sees how to rectify his mistake at once. So much importance does Montessori attach to this self-correction that she actually says that plastic work with clay, though included by her in the course followed by the children, is not educative, because it does not provide any means of making the children recognize their errors for themselves.

It is obvious that a method like this calls for a quite different conception of discipline from that which usually prevails in home and school. Children are generally forced to behave by the imposition of a veto on their activities; but this, Montessori thinks, is a quite wrong view of discipline. It confuses immobility with goodness and activity with badness; whereas in the very nature of the case there can be no goodness without free and spontaneous action. Her alternative to the ordinary discipline of inactivity is an activity controlled and regulated by the children themselves : not immobility imposed from without, but immobility determined from within. It is her contention that this higher discipline comes of itself in the course of the daily life of the Children's Houses. The light furniture of the schoolroom is not fixed in any way, but, contrary to the common expectation, that does not involve a continual noise as the children move about. What happens is that they gradually learn to work at their little chairs and desks without making any noise with them. The possibility of disorder is sufficient to call forth a spontaneous effort to maintain order. The unforced learning of the lesson-hour has a similar effect. The interest the children take in their work leads them to concentrate on what they are doing, and they come to control themselves as they would never do if they were compelled to learn what they did not want to learn. The practice of fixing attention on congenial occupations and resisting the temptation to turn aside to other things produces in course of time the habit of self-control.

Maria Montessori

The indirect influences of the school life are fortified by various exercises for the cultivation of voluntary immobility. The most notable of these are the games of silence, invented by Montessori herself. Here is one given in connexion with the tests for acuteness of hearing : " I call the children's attention to myself, telling them to see how silent I can be. I assume different positions . . . and maintain each pose silently without movement. . . . I call a child and ask him to do as I am doing. He adjusts his foot to an easier position and this makes a noise ! He moves his arm, stretching it out upon the arm of the chair, and it is a noise. His breathing is not altogether silent; it is not absolutely unheard as mine is. During these manœuvres the other children are watching and listening. Then they strive to imitate me and to do even better. . . . There is established a silence very different from that which we carelessly call by that name. It seems as if life gradually vanishes and that the room becomes little by little empty. Having arrived at that point, we darken the windows and tell the children to close their eyes, resting their heads upon their hands." Montessori then goes into a room behind the children and summons them softly to come to her, one by one. " This game," she adds, " delights the little ones beyond measure. Their intent faces, their patient immobility, reveal the enjoyment of a great pleasure." [1]

[1] *The Montessori Method*, pp. 209–211.

From Locke to Montessori

In accordance with the idea that freedom implies independence of the services of other people, Montessori gives an important place to what she calls the exercises of practical life in the daily routine of the children. They are taught to dress themselves and keep themselves clean, to dust and sweep the room, to look after the school apparatus, to set and serve the lunch, and to be courteous in their behaviour to their fellows. The youngest children begin with exercises in lacing, buttoning, hooking, and other operations required in dressing, and learn to move their chairs and tables without any noise. At the next stage they are taught to rise and to be seated in silence, and made to step along a chalk line on the floor to teach them to walk properly. Up to this point they get help in washing and dressing from the older children, but they are made to realize by example and precept that it is far better to be able to do these things for themselves. Consequently, when they grow a little older they take delight in attending to their own toilet, and they learn to handle all kinds of objects without doing any injury to them. Then finally they are entrusted with more responsible work. They are taught to make the room tidy and are allowed to serve out the meals to their little companions. The care of the person becomes more minute: they are shown how to wash their ears and their eyes, and taught to keep their teeth and mouths clean.

Maria Montessori

Other occupations akin to these, which, though of less obvious personal utility, help to cultivate the capacity for independent action, are those connected with the cultivation of the ground and the care of plants and animals, and the making of vases and brick structures with potter's clay.[1]

The method followed in teaching the children the domestic arts is to prepare for the more complex actions by a preliminary training in more elementary forms of them. The didactic apparatus by which they learn the various fastenings of dress as soon as they come to school exemplifies this well. It consists of a number of wooden frames, on each of which are mounted two pieces of cloth or leather, which have to be fastened and unfastened. There are altogether ten of these frames in use in the Children's Houses, illustrating all the common processes in dressing and undressing. " Through the use of such toys," comments Montessori, " the children can practically analyse the movements necessary in dressing and undressing themselves, and can prepare themselves separately for these movements by means of these exercises. We succeed in teaching

[1] It is difficult to see what *logical* place these occupations have in Dr Montessori's scheme. They are no doubt excellent forms of educational activity, the plastic work especially, but they have no obvious connexion with her principles, even if they are not inconsistent with them, as she herself seems at times to suspect (p. 163). Probably they owe their inclusion in her scheme to her eclectic regard for any form of work that gives promise of calling forth interest and provoking self-activity.

the child to dress himself without his really being aware of it—that is, without any direct or arbitrary command we have led him to this mastery." [1]

The same principle is applied in teaching the children to do all the exercises of practical life. The child who carries a tureen of soup across the floor has already mastered the separate actions required. He has learned to walk steadily along a fixed line and has acquired the ability to grasp things with his hands. The result is that the command to carry the soup which another child without this training would fail to execute, not because he was unwilling but because he was unable, is followed in his case by a ready obedience. Obedience, which other educators demand from children but do not get, is obtained as a matter of course by Montessori's method of showing the children *how* to obey.

It is sometimes said that self-education is the master principle of the Montessori system; but it is doubtful whether Dr Montessori herself would accept this as an adequate statement of the essential features of her method. It is quite true that she insists on the child doing his learning as far as possible without adult help or interference, and prescribes freedom as the general condition of all true education; but this insistence on free activity, though fundamental, does not and cannot indicate what is

[1] *The Montessori Method*, p. 146.

distinctive about the system. Freedom, as Montessori defines it, is a negative idea. When employed as a pedagogical principle it leads to the prohibition of certain methods of education, but does not in itself give any guidance as to what should be taught. Even when interpreted as social independence it continues vague and not very helpful. Independence, in spite of the suggestion it conveys of positive characters, is really a negative term, and has the uncertainty of implication which attaches to all negative terms. In practice it needs to draw meaning from the particular form of dependence that is in question. There is no knowledge or skill of any kind which might not conceivably be necessary for an independent life in some circumstances. It is not enough, therefore, to say that education should have freedom as its condition and independence as its goal. That does not tell us what education itself is. For that we must have some positive idea either of the process of growth in the child or of the ultimate aim in terms of adult life. In the Montessori system this is supplied by the conception of the child's development which Dr Montessori believed herself to have derived from Seguin, as beginning with muscular movements and from that going on to all kinds of sensory activity. The phrase which, according to her, sums up Seguin's aim and her own is this : " To lead the child as it were by the hand from the education of the muscular system to that of the nervous system and of the senses." [1] Later education involves a sequence of stages, to quote Montessori's quotation of Seguin, " from the education of the senses to general notions, from general notions to abstract thought, from abstract thought to morality "; but the beginning of the process, and for the teacher of young children the most important part of the process, is the training of the body and of the senses.

As a matter of fact this serial view of mental development is not Seguin's view at all, in spite of the quotations from him in which Montessori sets it forth. All through his discussion of education, Seguin, while laying himself open to the misunderstanding of which Montessori is guilty by stating development to be a succession of stages, is most careful to say that it is only the limitations of speech which force him to mark off one stage from another, and that really the whole nature of the individual who is being educated is directly affected at every stage. He is most careful to urge that a muscle or a sense should never be trained in detachment from the general functioning of mind. If detachment is necessary, as he admits it is in some cases, he would not allow it to be more than temporary. Once a capacity of any kind is acquired, it must be converted into a faculty and made part of the whole personality. These qualifications of the doctrine of serial

[1] *The Montessori Method,* p. 40.

development almost entirely disappear in Montessori's statement of it. She recognizes in general terms that the training of body has ultimately a value for the life of spirit, but in practice she concentrates attention on the training of each single function without any concern about its place in the whole physical and mental activity. Her view of development is not only not Seguin's view, but a view which Seguin would certainly have repudiated as contrary to his conception of the unity of human nature.

There is no need to enter into a discussion of this view of Montessori's at present. The point to be noted, before we go on to consider her methods of muscular and sensory training based on it, is that it is as fundamental an element in the whole system as the doctrine of freedom. The disciple of Montessori must subscribe not merely to a general faith in self-education, but accept the particular view of mental development in terms of which Montessori interprets it.

MOTOR EDUCATION

Montessori agrees with Seguin in attaching great importance to muscular training as part of the early education of children, and follows the lines laid down by him in working out her course of training. But though there is a general correspondence

From Locke to Montessori

between their systems, there is no part of her
scheme which shows more plainly how entirely she
differs from him in principle. For Seguin bodily
movement is a psychical fact, bound up with the
cycle of mental processes which begins with sense-
perception and only reaches its completion when
will manifests itself in muscular activities. For the
most part Montessori shows no consciousness of this
relation between the senses and movement. She
thinks of the senses and the muscles as two groups
of organs which develop independently, and regards
muscular activity as merely physiological in character. "We must understand by gymnastics and in
general by muscular education a series of exercises
tending to aid the normal development of physiological movements (such as walking, breathing,
speech), to protect this development when the child
shows himself backward or abnormal in any way,
and to encourage in the children those movements
which are useful in the achievement of the most
ordinary acts of life, such as dressing, undressing,
carrying such objects as balls, cubes, etc." [1] The
reason given for paying attention to muscular education is in keeping with her whole view. "A child,"
she says, "is characterized by having a torso greatly
developed in comparison with the lower limbs. . . .
If the child is not strong, the erect position and
walking are really sources of fatigue for him, and

[1] *The Montessori Method*, p. 138.

154

the long bones of the lower limbs, yielding to the weight of the body, easily become deformed and usually bowed." There is not a word here, it is to be noted, about the effect on mind and character of a body which for any reason can only carry out imperfectly the behests of mind. The whole concern is with such corporeal facts as deformed legs. For all that is said, body and mind might be thought to be two entities as completely different as they are for the man in the street.

To promote the physical development of the child, Montessori advocates considerable use of special gymnastic apparatus, some of it adapted from Seguin, the rest of it her own invention. The principle underlying the use of the various pieces of apparatus is that they should give occasion for exercises corresponding to the movements which the individual child needs to make under normal conditions. She illustrates this by reference to the wire fence she recommends for use in children's playgrounds. In the course of her work in one of the Children's Houses she noticed that some of the younger children who grew tired of marching with the others often fell out of the ranks ; but instead of resting they climbed on to a fence which happened to be in the courtyard, and pulled themselves along the wires. Always ready to turn her observations of the children's doings to account, she recognized at once that they had solved one of her problems in a practical way. They had reduced the strain on their legs caused by the weight of the body, and yet had contrived to get the exercise they needed. The other pieces of apparatus included Seguin's swing, a little wooden staircase, a wooden platform adapted for the broad jump, and rope ladders, all of them constructed, like the wire fence, to provide the children with better outlets for individual activity than ordinary town life provides. In her judgment, gymnastic apparatus of this kind, when used intelligently, gives opportunity for the most varied exercises, and tends to establish the co-ordination of such common movements as walking, throwing, going up and down stairs, kneeling, rising, jumping, and the like.

In addition to exercises with apparatus, she makes considerable use of free gymnastics without any apparatus at all. She distinguishes two forms of such gymnastics : directed exercises and free games. About the games she does not say very much, probably because she does not estimate the educational value of games very highly. Her general attitude to games, at any rate, is rather contemptuous. When illustrating the fact that some adults of an inferior type resemble children, she includes games and what she calls 'foolish stories' in a common condemnation. In the light of this, the fact that she furnished the children in the Houses with balls, hoops, and kites and allowed

them to play simple games of their own is probably
to be regarded as a concession to their childishness
rather than a serious part of her plan. Even directed
exercises, though meeting with a more hearty
approval, do not play any large part in her scheme.
The only form chosen for special mention is marching, and it is characteristic of her conception of
muscular exercises that the benefits she anticipates
from it are purely physical. It is well to accompany
the march with little songs, she says, " because
this furnishes a breathing exercise very helpful in
strengthening the lungs." [1] She even goes out of her
way to depreciate any but the physical effects, by
stating expressly that the object of the marching
exercise should not be rhythm, but only poise. This
is a position very difficult to understand, even if
Montessori did not profess adherence to Seguin's
conception of education. Rhythm is one of the
most primitive impulses of children, and the pleasure
they take in marching proves it to be one of the most
fundamental of the psychical elements.

A related form of exercise is provided by what
Dr Montessori calls respiratory gymnastics, consisting of free gymnastics co-ordinated with breathing
exercises. The main purpose for which they are
given is to regulate the movements of respiration,
but they also serve to prepare for good articulation,
for which, indeed, further provision is made at a

[1] *The Montessori Method*, p. 144.

later time by means of special exercises in the use of lips, tongue, and teeth.

THE TRAINING OF THE SENSES

The great importance attached by Dr Montessori to the training of the senses is indicated by the fact that she designates the special apparatus she uses for the purpose *the* didactic system. The reason she gives for making this training so prominent in early education is the fundamental part played by the senses all through life. According to her, the nascence of sensory discrimination in its various forms from three to seven gives an opportunity to the educator of exercising a decisive influence on later development. If the senses are neglected in these years, the whole intellectual life of the adult is likely to be crippled. However intelligent a man may be, nothing he can do in after-years will altogether make up for the inability to discriminate accurately the different sense-stimuli. He may learn all that is to be known of the theory and practice of his trade or profession, but if his senses have been left untrained in the critical years of early childhood he will always fall short of complete efficiency by reason of a greater or less degree of sensory obtuseness.

To discuss with profit the apparatus employed by Dr Montessori in training the senses it is necessary to understand the principles that underlie the use of it.

Maria Montessori

(1) The general character of sense-education is thus defined by her: "The education of the senses has as its aim the refinement of the differential perception of stimuli by means of repeated exercises." [1] What is sought is not to give the child *knowledge* of any kind about his environment with regard to sense-perceived objects, nor even to connect these objects with their names. The connexion between nomination and concrete ideas on the one hand and sensory experiences on the other is, and should be, very intimate; but the sensory experience must have the priority. First sensory discrimination, then almost immediately thereafter the fixing of the perceived distinction in language, and at a later time the understanding of what is perceived: that is the right order. Montessori illustrates her view by referring to the three periods into which Seguin divided his lessons. (*a*) The association of the sensory perception with the name. A red article, for example, is put before the child, and he is told, "This is red"; then a blue, and he is told, "This is blue." (*b*) Recognition of the name corresponding to the object. We say to the child, "Give me the red"; then, "Give me the blue." (*c*) The remembering of the name of the object. When asked, "What is this?" the child should say, "Red" or "Blue," as the case may be. Montessori approves of this sequence, and follows it

[1] *The Montessori Method*, p. 173.

in her own practice. But she thinks that in the case of normal children there is another stage preceding these three, during which the real sense-training is going on, through the acquisition of a fineness of differential perception. In the discrimination of colours, for example, she wants her pupils to be able to grade eight different colours in eight different shades; in doing which they are bound to acquire a delicacy of appreciation greater than they can express in words either at this or even it may be at any later age. So again in the exercises into which geometrical figures enter, there is no intention to teach the children geometry. They begin by distinguishing the various figures through touch and sight, then learn their names, and only after a considerable time undertake the simple analysis implied in knowing the names of their constituent parts.

(2) The education of the senses must in the nature of the case be auto-education. Just as no teacher can furnish the child with the agility he acquires from a gymnastic training, so no one but himself can ever gain for him the power of fine sensory discrimination. All education worthy of the name implies personal exertion, no doubt, but in the more intellectual forms of learning the teacher can make the way easier for the pupil by doing some of his thinking for him. The perceptive process, however, which is mainly concerned in the training

of the senses, is essentially individual. The child must hear or see or touch for himself, or his senses will remain undeveloped. The art of sense-training therefore consists in inducing the pupil to undertake his own training by the supply of materials that call forth and exercise his personal activities. This is achieved in Dr Montessori's system by means of the didactic apparatus. This apparatus in all its varieties has (or is intended to have) one common feature. It always involves an interesting exercise, with the possibility of errors which reveal themselves to the child in the result and lead him to make the attempt to correct himself. Take, for example, the first object given to the little ones—a block of wood with holes in it into which a series of ten different wooden cylinders have to be fitted exactly. The child gets the cylinders in a heap, and is required to sort them out by sight or touch, or by sight and touch combined, and put them in their proper place in the block. Any mistake in the choice of a cylinder, either in taking one too large or one too small, becomes evident as soon as he tries to put them all into the holes, and leads to fresh trials till they all occupy their own places. There is no need for the intervention of the teacher at any point in the exercise. When the child has been given the apparatus and shown what to do with it, the inherent interest of the task and the obvious consequences of errors lead him to maintain the effort which is necessary for a successful result. Once that is accomplished he is at liberty to repeat the exercise or to go on to a new one as he feels disposed. The object of it is to train his senses, not to give him complete mastery of the apparatus. The absence of interest is taken to indicate that he has learned all he can from it and is ready for some new venture.

(3) In the training of the several senses one or two guiding rules are observed. One is that each sense should be made capable of doing its work in independence of the others, in order that the ultimate development of them all may be as complete as possible. Under ordinary conditions, when no training has been given, the pre-eminence of vision is so great that the rest of the senses are unable to attain their maximum of efficiency. Touch in particular, which is one of the earliest to mature, and which is capable of a surprising degree of accuracy when trained, is apt to remain comparatively impotent. With a view to the general development of the senses, blindfold exercises are necessary. They delight the children and give the happiest results. Another important rule is that the training of a sense should generally begin with the presentation of sharply contrasted objects—for example, with colours like red and blue, or with the darkest and lightest shades of a colour—and that gradually the degree of contrast should be diminished

until the child is able to distinguish minute differences and to appreciate series of graded stimuli.

The Didactic Apparatus.—The didactic apparatus consists of twenty-six different items, and makes provision for the training of all the senses except taste and smell. This training begins when the child enters school about three. He is then given wooden cylinders to fit into holes in a solid block of wood. This, it is to be noted, is intended to be an exercise for vision. If the order of biological development had been followed the sense to be first exercised would have been touch. But the simple sensations of touch are not the first to attract the child's attention. Hence the beginning with the more complex as well as more interesting exercises with the solid insets. Of these there are three. In each case there is a block of wood with holes in it for ten cylindrical pieces, much after the fashion of the case of weights used with the chemical balance. In the first and easiest the cylinders are all of the same height but decrease in diameter, in the second there is a gradual decrease both in height and diameter, while in the third (which is the most difficult of all) the diameters are the same but the height decreases. As the child goes on playing with these insets he gets his first experience of dimensions, and learns to differentiate objects according to thickness, height, and size.

At the second stage this training in the perception

of dimensions is continued with larger objects which require more difficult movements and greater muscular effort. These are the cubes, the big stair, and the long stair. The cubes, which are rose-coloured, are ten in number, the largest having a 10-cm. side, the next largest a 9-cm. side, and so down to the smallest, with a side of 1 cm. These are used by the younger children in the construction of a tower with the largest cube at the bottom, and suggest the distinction of *larger* and *smaller* objects. The big stair is built up from ten rectangular blocks, stained dark brown, all of them 20 cm. long, but with bases decreasing from 10 cm. to 1 cm. Attention is called by it to distinctions of *thickness* and *thinness*. The long stair is constructed with ten rods, all the same thickness of 3 cm., but varying regularly in length from a metre to a decimetre. Each space of one decimetre on them is painted alternately red and blue, and they have to be so arranged that the colours correspond and form a series of transverse strips. This construction, though very attractive, presents considerable difficulty to most children, and is only accomplished after the other two have been mastered. Its first object is to teach appreciation of *length*, but at a later time it is of great value in arithmetical work.

Once the child has reached this point in his education he is capable of taking an interest in thermic and tactile stimuli. The training of the senses of heat and touch go together, since warmth renders the sense of touch more acute. For the thermic training the hands are put in cold, luke-warm, and hot water to get contrasts of cold and heat, and at a later time a series of metal bowls filled with water at various temperatures is em-ployed to give graded impressions of heat. The tactile exercises begin with a lesson in the right method of touching, by passing the finger-tips lightly over the surface to be examined. In addi-tion to touching various materials with the eyes shut, there are more formal lessons with the didactic apparatus, which consists of a tablet covered with alternating strips of smooth paper and sandpaper, and of a rectangular wooden board divided into two equal rectangles, one covered with smooth paper or having the wood polished smooth, the other covered with sandpaper.

At the same time as the thermic and tactile trainings are going on a beginning is made with the training of the chromatic sense. The first exercise here is the pairing of colours. Pieces of coloured stuffs or balls of coloured wool may be used, but generally it is flat tablets wound with coloured wool or silk which form the didactic material. Three strong colours, like red, blue, and yellow, are placed before the child in a heap that contains two tablets of each colour, and he is required to find the duplicates and arrange them in a row two by two.

From Locke to Montessori

This exercise is made increasingly difficult by adding to the number of colours and using lighter shades.

At the third stage in sense-training the child is introduced to gradations of those stimuli with which he has already become acquainted. For the discernment of various degrees of roughness and smoothness, for example, he is presented with a collection of paper strips, varying through many grades from smooth cardboard to the coarsest sandpaper. Fine distinctions in colour are learned by means of the colour tablets, the complete set of which consists of sixty-four spools, giving eight colours in eight shades. The child learns to pair any one of these with its duplicate in another set, and to arrange each group of eight shades in its proper order.

The training of the sense of hearing and of the sense of weight is now begun. So far as hearing goes, the didactic method, on Montessori's confession, really breaks down, because it is not possible for the child to exercise himself through his own activity in hearing as he does for the other senses. Nevertheless, the attempt is made to educate the ear to distinguish noises from sounds, and to discern the character of particular sounds and noises. For the gradation of noises small boxes filled with such substances as sand and pebbles are employed. The child has to estimate the size of their contents from the noise they make when shaken. For the precise discrimination of sounds there is a series of little whistles. One of the difficulties of these and other exercises for the training of the ear is that absolute silence is necessary. This is partly met by the games of silence. A deep silence is gradually produced in the class-room, and the children are invited to listen to such sounds as the buzzing of the flies and the rustling of the trees. Then a succession of different sounds and noises is produced, beginning with strong contrasts and gradually becoming more nearly alike.

The material for the training of the baric sense consists of little wooden tablets of the same size, made of different kinds of wood, and weighing respectively 24, 18, and 12 grammes. The child takes one in each hand at the base of the outstretched fingers, and moves his hands up and down to gauge their relative weights. With this training in the discrimination of weights goes the education of the stereognostic sense, in which the tactile and the muscular senses are simultaneously brought into play to distinguish objects of different shapes.

At the same time as the training in the gradation of stimuli is going on the training of the sense of form is effected by means of flat wooden insets of various geometrical shapes, which can be fitted into corresponding spaces. A number of different insets with their frames are placed in a rectangular tray, and the insets are then taken out and mixed on the

From Locke to Montessori

table. The child has to replace each one in its proper frame, guided by the fact that he cannot put a triangular inset, for example, into a square or a circular frame, or indeed into any frame except the one from which it was originally taken. In this exercise recognition is partly a matter of vision and partly a matter of touch and muscular sensation. Many children who find difficulty in matching insets and frames from merely seeing them appreciate the difference of form when they have passed the index finger of the hand round the contrasted objects. Hence in this exercise the pupils are encouraged to make a practice of examining the contours of the insets and the related spaces, so as to associate the impression of the muscular-tactile sense with that of vision. This, it is found, makes for the accurate perception of forms and helps to fix them in the memory.

After the wooden insets can be put in the frames without difficulty the children are exercised in the recognition of the geometrical forms with three sets of cards on which the same forms are presented in an increasingly abstract way. On the first set the whole figure appears in blue paper pasted on a white background. On the second there is only a contour of the figure with the outside boundary a centimetre in width, again in blue paper. On the third the figure is represented by a simple line. The game for the child is to recognize the correspondence of these cardboard figures with the wooden ones, and to show it by covering up each cardboard figure with a wooden one. The training in form is complete when the child understands the representation of objects by means of the simple line. This part of his education begins with form in its most concrete aspects as it manifests itself in solid bodies. From that he passes to form in two dimensions, and finally he reaches forms as represented abstractly by lines.

In the fourth stage of sensory training the only new feature is the training of the ear to recognize musical sounds. The apparatus for this purpose consists of a double series of thirteen bells, which produce an ascending sequence of musical tones on being struck with a hammer. Having struck one of the bells in the first series, the child is required to find the corresponding sound in the second series. This exercise, Montessori admits, is not a success. The children cannot strike the bells with constant force, and even when the teacher strikes them they have difficulty in distinguishing between one sound and another.

At this stage all the earlier exercises are repeated, generally in the form of games, and the children begin to generalize their sense experiences by applying the words which have in the first instance been associated with the didactic material to objects in the world around them. This, like the more formal sensory education of which it is the continuation, is left to await the natural development of the child; and even when the child seems to be rather backward no attempt is made to give him any direct lessons for a considerable time, it may be for months. With normal children there usually comes a spontaneous outburst of the spirit of exploration. Suddenly the child will discover that the sky is blue or that the cloth of his dress is smooth, and then he wanders about full of delight, seeking fresh objects to which to apply the epithets he has learned in the course of his previous training.

WRITING AND READING

In the Montessori schools the learning of reading, writing, and arithmetic [1] follows immediately on the various exercises of the senses, and is, indeed, a direct development from them. When the Children's Houses were first established Dr Montessori had no intention of including these subjects in the course of training. She shared the general opinion of enlightened teachers that young children of the age of those with whom she had to deal were not mature enough for this kind of instruction. But experience led to a modification of this view, and she took it

---

[1] I have said nothing about the arithmetical methods of Montessori because they do not seem to me of any special value; the details about writing and reading give sufficient illustration of her principles in any case.

up, partly because her pupils were generally able to complete the course of sensory training she gave them before they were old enough to pass on to the ordinary school, partly because some of them wanted to learn their letters and were making attempts to do so on their own account. She was the more willing to make this addition to the curriculum because she had already been successful in teaching idiot children to read and write, and in doing so had hit on a method which admitted of ready adaptation to normal children with cultivated senses.

The manner of discovery is interesting, and throws light on the principle of the method. One of the idiots whom she was teaching, a girl of eleven, though quite strong and able to use her hands, could not learn to sew or even to darn. Noticing this, she set her to weave with the Froebel mats, in which a strip of paper is threaded transversely in and out among vertical strips of paper, by a series of movements similar to those required for darning, but on a larger scale. Then when the girl became skilful in this work she brought her back to the sewing, and found that she was now able to darn. This at once suggested to her a principle of far-reaching consequence. "I saw," she says, "that the necessary movements of the hand in sewing *had been prepared without having the child sew*, and that we should really find the way to *teach* the child *how* before *making him execute* a task. I saw especially that preparatory movements could be carried on and reduced to a mechanism by means of repeated exercises, not in the work itself, but in that which prepares for it." [1]

This was the idea that guided her experiments in the teaching of writing. She had already taught the children to touch the contours of the geometric insets. By a simple extension of this exercise she gave them the same intimate acquaintance with the forms of the written letters. She got the letters cut out in sandpaper, 8 cm. in height and $\frac{1}{2}$ cm. in breadth, and gummed on cardboard, and she made them pass their fingers over them with movements similar to those they would afterwards employ in writing. But she saw that in addition to this the children must learn to manipulate the pencil or the pen, since that requires a muscular action different from that of the writing movements. To that end she made them trace out the shape of various insets on paper and fill in the resulting figures with a coloured pencil held in the proper position for writing. As a rule the results of this are most satisfactory. The strokes, which at first are short and confused, become gradually longer and more nearly parallel, until in many cases the figures are filled in with perfectly regular up-and-down lines, and the child is obviously more familiar with

[1] *The Montessori Method*, p. 261.

Maria Montessori

the use of the pen than if he had filled many pages with pothooks. It is then time to establish the visual-muscular image of the letters and the muscular memory of the movements necessary for writing. The material for this consists of cards on which the letters of the alphabet are mounted singly in sand-paper, as well as larger cards with groups of the same letters. The teacher hands the child the letter, giving its sound, and the child passes the index finger of the right hand along it. The tracing movement is repeated a great many times, often with the eyes shut, until the form of the letter is thoroughly familiar. After the visual and the muscular-tactual sensations have been associated in this way with the sound of the letter the teacher asks the child for it by name, to see if he recognizes it when he hears its sound. The learning at this stage is completed when the child can give a correct answer to the question, " What letter is that ? " He is then on the way to be able to write and to read.

But he is not yet quite ready for either. He still requires to learn how to convert the words he hears into the form of script. As soon as he knows some of the vowels and consonants Montessori provides him with a box of letters identical in form and dimensions with those he has been using already, but cut out of cardboard and not mounted. In the box there is a fixed compartment for every letter, and there are four copies of each. The teacher

pronounces a word like 'mamma' very clearly,
taking care to bring out the consonant sound. After
some repetition the child generally connects it with
the single sound which he knows already, and picks
out the corresponding letter from the box and lays
it on the table. The same process is gone through
with the vowel following the consonant, and then
with the other parts of the word, until the letters
representing it lie out on the table. But that is
only half of the child's task : he has still to read the
whole word he has composed. To help him over the
new difficulty the teacher reads over the word once
or twice, until he sees that the combination of letters
has a meaning. Once that is realized he is able to
compose any word that is clearly pronounced, at
first very slowly and with an infinite number of
repetitions of the word he is making, but ultimately
with great ease and rapidity.

Up to this point the child has never written, but
he is now master of all the acts necessary for writing.
No attempt, however, is made to teach him writing,
at least for a very considerable time. He is left
to go on practising the separate actions, and if he
is an ordinarily intelligent child he breaks suddenly
into writing one day, and thenceforward finds no
difficulty in writing the names of any things he knows
about.[1] Perfect proficiency, it is needless to say,

[1] It must be remembered that the language of Dr Montessori's pupils
was Italian, the spelling of which is almost perfectly phonetic.

is not acquired at once. Generally the children go on repeating the preliminary exercises for some time after they have discovered the secret of writing, and they gradually improve on their first performance. But the spontaneous appearance of the ability to write is a critical point in their educational progress.

The results of the method recorded by Dr Montessori are certainly astonishing. In the case of four-year-old children the average time that elapses between the first trial of the preparatory exercises and the first written word is from a month to six weeks. With children of five the period is shorter. As for execution, the children write well from the first. The form of the letters is surprisingly like that of the sandpaper models. The ordinary writing of even older children in the schools of any country compares unfavourably with that of Montessori's pupils.

The method of teaching reading followed in the Children's Houses has not the same originality as the method of teaching writing. But there is an original idea underlying it which is worthy of attention—viz., that reading should be taught after writing, and not before it, as is commonly done. The reason Montessori gives for this order is that children can put together the letters constituting a word much more easily than they can grasp the significance of the words once they are formed. In writing they are translating a succession of sounds into a succession of symbols ; but in reading they have the more difficult task of comprehending words as a whole, and relating them to the objects they denote. Her method of teaching reading takes this difference into account. She writes in large, clear script on ordinary writing-paper, or on cards, the names of well-known objects which have already been pronounced several times by the pupils. The child is shown one of these cards and asked to name the sounds of the written letters. At first he utters them too slowly to apprehend the word as a whole, and he is urged to speak faster. As soon as he does so the sounds coalesce into a word, and the meaning becomes evident. He thereupon puts the card under the object whose name it bears and the exercise is complete. Following on this and confirming the lesson is a game, in which the child gets a toy to play with when he can read the card on which its name is written.

Once the children are able to read words Montessori proceeds to teach phrases by similar methods and with similar results. In this case also the principle that writing precedes reading in order of mental development received demonstration from experience. On one occasion, early in the history of the Children's Houses, picture-books were sent to Montessori by friends for the use of the school, and against her own judgment she allowed the teachers to put them into the hands of the children. The children, rejoicing in their ability to read words,

Maria Montessori

seemed to read the books quite fluently. But on cross-examination they showed that they had no real comprehension of the meaning of what they had been reading. It was not till they had spontaneously burst into composition, as they had previously burst into the writing of words, that they learned to put meaning into the words they wrote and really read with understanding.

Dr Montessori, it should be added, does not attach as much importance to writing and reading as many of the readers of her book. " After years of applying the method with a great number of normal children, she is almost convinced that it is not natural for children under six, unless they are over-stimulated, either to read or to write continuously."[1] For her part, she regards the literary arts as a by-product of her method rather than as one of its substantial results, and is more concerned that the children should go forward to the later years of school life with well-developed senses than that they should be expert in writing and reading.

BIBLIOGRAPHICAL NOTE

Dr Montessori has published two volumes, *Antropologia Pedagogica* and *Il Metodo della Pedagogia Scientifica applicato all' Educazione Infantile nelle Case dei Bambini*, both of which have been translated into English. The latter has been published, with additions and amendments, under the title

[1] Miss Tozier: *The Montessori Apparatus* in *The World's Work*, March, 1912.

From Locke to Montessori

of *The Montessori Method*. A considerable number of articles and books about the system, both expository and critical, have appeared during the last two years. The most helpful of these are : Miss Tozier's articles in *The Fortnightly Review*, August 1911, and in *The World's Work*, February and March 1912 ; *The Montessori System*, by E. G. A. Holmes (English Board of Education) ; *The Montessori System*, by Dr Theodate L. Smith ; *A Montessori Mother*, by Mrs Fisher (an excellent book) ; *The Montessori Method*, by Dr S. A. Morgan (Ontario Department of Education) ; *A Guide to the Montessori Method*, by Ellen Y. Stevens ; *Montessori Principles and Practice*, by Professor Culverwell. *The Demonstration School Record* (Manchester University), No. II, states the results of work done with the Montessori material in the Fielden School, and gives references to similar work done elsewhere.

PART II—CRITICAL

CHAPTER VIII

THE MONTESSORI POINT OF VIEW

TO any one who is acquainted with the history of education and knows about the waxing and waning of methods which in their own times enjoyed a great repute, there must be some serious doubts as to the future of the Montessori system. Naturally enough, Dr Montessori and her disciples are not troubled with such misgivings. She herself has visions of a time when her schools will be planted all over the world, with Raphael's 'Madonna of the Chair' on their walls to recall the land of their origin and the spirit of their founder ; and even less sanguine supporters, who are conscious of the power of vested educational interests and prejudices, are quite convinced of the eternal value of the system and determined to do all that they can to make it the basis of civilized education. Is their faith justified ?

In discussing this question it is necessary to distinguish between the actual method as embodied in the apparatus and practices of the schools and what may be called the Montessori principles. For those

179

who have accepted the system as a great new discovery the two, indeed, are inseparable. They see the principles becoming effective through the apparatus and the apparatus getting its significance from the principles, and they regard them in their conjunction as an organic whole. But if the history of thought makes one thing clearer than another, it is that principles of any kind only become a permanent factor in the advance of the human spirit by shedding the forms in which they first gained recognition. There are many such cases in educational experience. Pestalozzi, to take a not very remote example, spent a lifetime in striving to give practical effect to a new idea, and even in the day of his greatest success was conscious that all he could say or do fell far short of the fullness of his conception. We have discarded the greater part of his system in its original form, but his idea still determines in large measure what is best in all our systems.

Should we be asked then about the future of the Montessori method, we must have it made clear to us whether the question refers to the method as we actually see it at work under the most favourable conditions and nearest to the mind of its founder, or to the ruling ideas of the method, which can only be imperfectly realized in practice under any conditions, but are capable of progressive development toward complete realization. If, as the advocates of the

The Montessori Point of View

system are likely to maintain (and ought to maintain if their advocacy is worth anything), the claim to permanence is made on behalf of the working method, and we are called on to contemplate the possibility of the persistence of the kind of relation between teachers and pupils which Montessori prescribes, and of the continued use of the special apparatus which she has invented, we may reasonably express the frankest scepticism. Such things do not happen in the sphere of education. The only articles of long standing in the schoolroom are the abacus and the rod, and both of them have fallen considerably in repute in these latter days. The Froebelian gifts, which are most like the didactic apparatus in general character, do not furnish an encouraging parallel. There are few schools in any part of the world where the gifts are used as Froebel meant them to be used ; the best kindergartens are conducted in the spirit of the master, but those responsible for their management are usually very indifferent followers of his practice. Seguin's apparatus, again, which Montessori has rescued from an undeserved oblivion by reconstructing its most valuable pieces for her own purposes, affords an even more direct refutation of any pretensions to finality on the part of the advocates of the Montessori system.

There is always the possibility, of course, that a particular method may escape the common fate.

From Locke to Montessori

Perhaps the Montessori method may be such an exception. If, like the Morse code or Pitman's phonography or Esperanto or some similar invention, it were a great social convenience and met a fundamental need of human life unsatisfied or imperfectly satisfied before, then the chances of survival would be much greater. But is there any reason whatever for imputing to it such an uncommon character? Even if it be granted that no proper provision is made for sensory training in ordinary education and that such training is really essential to complete development, is the didactic apparatus so entirely satisfactory a means of making good the defect that it would be desirable to use it in the education of all children and to go on using it generation after generation? One would need to be a very blind admirer of Dr Montessori and her work to believe this.

Without following this speculative line of argument further at present, it may be assumed that if the Montessori school of to-day is destined to survive at all it will very probably change even in those respects which seem to its adherents to be most distinctive. There still remains the possibility that its passing may be a dying to live, and that the ideas which have brought it into existence and given it the power to influence the current of educational thought may be set free for a wider usefulness. Here prophecy is on less sure ground. Whether there is any prospect of future life for the principles underlying the Montessori system it is difficult to say. Everything depends on the value of these principles. It will be well to reserve judgment until we have examined them and seen what they imply.

Venturing to be more definite than Dr Montessori herself, we may indicate three main ideas as the foundations of her educational practice. The first is the principle of individuality : that each person manifests in a unique way the mysterious life-force and attains to the most complete realization of his own possibilities by following the direction given by his individual impulses. The second, which is in some sense deducible from the first, is the principle of freedom : that the individual in maturing his powers and becoming adapted to social life through education develops best in the absence of conventional restrictions on his individuality. The third is the psychological doctrine which makes the senses the basis of the higher life of man and requires their cultivation in early childhood as the precondition of complete success in later education. Taken together, these ideas may be said to constitute the Montessori point of view.[1]

[1] One might perhaps add as a fourth principle the need for 'socializing the maternal functions' by the creation of such institutions as the Children's Houses. If this is really an essential part of Dr Montessori's creed, as it seems to be, it is of subordinate importance to the other principles.

From Locke to Montessori

It may be urged by any one disposed to be critical of Dr Montessori's claims that no one of these ideas is in any way peculiar to her. The emphasis on the individuality which reveals itself in impulse is one of the commonest notes in post-Darwinian philosophy. It appears in particular in the exaltation of will over intellect, which is equally characteristic of pragmatism and of present-day psychology. The demand for freedom, again, has been made by nearly every notable educational thinker for the last two hundred years. Not to mention Rousseau (whom Montessori underrates) or any of his followers, all of them as much convinced as she of the need for free development, there has been complete anticipation of all that she says on behalf of freedom in Tolstoy. It would be impossible, indeed, for any one to preach or to practise the method of freedom more thoroughly than he. As for the doctrine of the priority of the senses in growth and training, there also Montessori has had many predecessors. It is sufficient to refer to the *Emile* to show that she has no new principles to impart to the world on that subject.

It may even be urged, though here some qualification would perhaps be necessary, that the combination of the three principles by Montessori is not new. Reference to the historical survey in Part I will show that they are all adumbrated in Locke and that they are explicitly enunciated by

The Montessori Point of View

Rousseau. Indeed, it may be said that, apart from details of method, there is none of Montessori's principles which is not to be found in more adequate form in Rousseau.

So far, however, from this lack of originality being a weakness of Montessori's case, it constitutes its real strength. Originality in the sense of complete novelty of idea is neither necessary nor desirable in the reconstruction of social institutions. A scheme of education having behind it ideas like individuality and freedom, which are the master principles of democracy, and a psychological theory of long standing supported by medical experience, has a great advantage in dynamic over the most plausible notions devised by a *tour de force* of individual invention. Originality in practical matters is more properly exhibited in the discovery and elaboration of new applications of principles already accepted in their vague generality. The concrete interpretation of an old idea in a new practice or method is a genuine addition to the sum of human wisdom. It always involves to some extent the reshaping and development of the idea and the revelation of unexpected meanings and values.

That Montessori has enriched the principles which have come to her by inheritance not merely from her educational predecessors but from the spirit of the age is not to be denied. One has only to compare

From Locke to Montessori

her educational scheme with that of Rousseau from the practical point of view to appreciate the value of her contribution to educational thought and practice. Rousseau, with a conception of education fundamentally identical with hers, evades all the difficulties of educational work by expounding his methods with reference to the exceptional case of a child in a very uncommon situation. In spite of the fact that his ideals are implicitly democratic, the practical proposals he puts forward would only be feasible if education were restricted to an aristocratic few. Montessori, living in an age that makes greater demands on its idealists, could not escape the difficulties of converting her theories into practical forms in this easy and unsatisfactory way. She had to face, and did face, the modern problem of educating all the children of all the people ; and it is her distinction as an educator that she has succeeded within the limits of the infant years in providing a solution which is consistent in the main with the requirements of individual freedom. Even if, as it seems to me, the conception of social relations which is implied in her attempt overrates the individual factors in education and underrates the social, the fact remains that she has devised a method of education which takes account of individuality in the daily routine of the school. That is an achievement of first-rate importance on any view of her system. It involves a definite advance in the conception of education as essentially individual, of which we have followed the gradual development from the time of Locke. With her schools in being, educational individualism passes beyond the stage of mere criticism and theoretical illustration, and compels the attention which is always due to the accomplished fact.

It may be that neither Montessori nor any one else is capable of extending her method beyond the early years of life. It is undoubtedly in these years from birth to the age of six or seven, with which she has mainly concerned herself up to this time, that an individualistic method can be most easily employed without personal development coming into overt conflict with social claims ; and it is possible that any kind of school for children in later childhood requires to restrict individuality in a fashion incompatible with her principles.[1] She herself, however, does not anticipate any insuperable difficulties in the extension of her system, and is, indeed, busy at the attempt to carry forward her work into the later stages of school life.

It is conceivable that she may fail ; but whether she succeeds or fails the need will remain for the

[1] Mr Holmes is quite convinced from his own acquaintance with the work of 'Egeria' in an English country school that there is no age-limit to a method based on freedom (see his book, *What is and what might be*). Tolstoy's extraordinary school at Yásnaya Polyána is also worthy of consideration in this connexion. *Cf.* his *Pedagogical Articles* (Dent).

ordinary school to find means of giving the freedom requisite for the best education of the individual child. For, considered broadly, the problem with which she is dealing is not peculiar to her or to those people who hold an educational view like hers. In some form or other, it is the standing problem of democratic education. With political institutions like ours, requiring for their successful working an intelligent populace, it is intolerable that the children who are to be the citizens of the future should continue to be educated under conditions that tend to discourage initiative and to minimise individuality. It is imperative in the interests both of the community and its members that some practical reconciliation of individual needs and social demands should be effected by means of a right organization of the whole system of education. And even if we cannot accept Montessori's methods in their entirety or even to any considerable extent, we must devise methods of some kind which will do greater justice to legitimate individuality than those which she criticizes. In that reconstruction of our educational system we shall almost certainly find that there is much to be learned from the theory and practice of Montessori and her predecessors.

We have now to go on to examine the leading principles underlying the Montessori methods. From what has been already said it will be evident that the real interest of the discussion is not in the

The Montessori Point of View

merits and the demerits of Dr Montessori's scheme, though that provides a text for the discussion, but in the value of the point of view which it pre-supposes. For that reason we shall try as far as possible to avoid dwelling on defects which are incidental to Dr Montessori's exposition and seek to get to a proper understanding of her central ideas at their best. Only by doing so shall we be able to derive from the study of what is, on the lowest estimate, a genuine educational experiment some guidance in the search for a fuller solution of the educational problem of to-day.

CHAPTER IX

INDIVIDUALITY

"THE educator," says Dr Montessori, in a passage which deserves the most careful scrutiny for the light that it throws on her philosophical prepossessions, "must be as one inspired by a deep *worship of life*, and must, through this reverence, *respect*, while he observes with human interest the *development* of the child life. Now, child life is not an abstraction; *it is the life of individual children*. There exists only one real biological manifestation : *the living individual ;* and towards single individuals, one by one observed, education must direct itself." [1] In this passage, it will be noted, the very ambiguous idea of individuality is expressly defined in biological terms. We are invited to understand the individuality of a child as we would understand the individuality of a dog or a cat. In man, as in the other animals, environment produces profound modifications of the original nature. But environment is only a

[1] *The Montessori Method*, p. 104. The profusion of italics in this passage is worthy of attention for the indication it gives of the unscientific temper of Montessori's mind. It reveals the glowing faith of a devotee or the sentiment of a romancer rather than the critical attitude of a scientist.

Individuality

secondary factor in the phenomena of life. The essential characteristics which constitute individuality are those which are present from the beginning in the germ cell, and which, in spite of the modifications due to the particular experiences of the individual man or animal, are transmitted without change to the next generation. " The child," Montessori insists, " does not grow *because* he is nourished, *because* he breathes, *because* he is placed in conditions of temperature to which he is adapted ; he grows because the potential life within him develops, making itself visible ; because the fruitful germ from which his life has come develops itself according to the biological destiny which was fixed for it by heredity."

In spite of the scientific guise in which it is decked, this is just the old Stoic doctrine of the man of nature, man in himself as opposed to man fashioned and shaped by society, which has been resurrected in every age of transition as a criterion to be applied in the judgment of existing institutions ; and it is open to all the objections which make that doctrine untenable. The implication is that human nature can be defined quite adequately, apart from its social manifestations, in terms of certain original impulses : otherwise, of course, there would be no standard by which to approve or to condemn these social manifestations. But, in point of fact, it is only man as made

From Locke to Montessori

by society that we know. The natural man, the original nature unmodified by education, are mere abstractions, hypotheses parading as facts. Montessori, it is true, seems to evade this objection by making no attempt to define the original characteristics of humanity. Her contention is that behind the individual human being is the mysterious life-force that defines itself in the process of growth, and does so all the better if we refrain from trying to determine the manner of its growing by our definitions. But this unscientific resort to mystery is really a surrender of the biological conception of humanity. It is tantamount to an admission that we cannot know the original human characters, but are limited in our knowledge to the social forms in which the life-force clothes itself in the case of man. Some of these may be good and some bad, but which are good and which bad, and what goodness and badness mean in this connexion, there is nothing in this pseudo-biological conception of an incomprehensible force to tell us.

However that be, the fact remains that Montessori makes a sharp distinction between the biological and the social elements in human nature, and seeks to define individuality in terms of the former. Individuality is for her a characteristic of life itself, and it shares in the mystic sanctity with which for some occult reason she regards life as invested. The

Individuality

living individual, simply because he is a living individual, seemingly has rights against all social institutions, from the least to the greatest. The first duty of any human being is to be himself, and anything that infringes his natural liberties and prevents him living his own life does him the most serious injustice.

Applied logically, this is a revolutionary doctrine. It cuts right across the conventional social grades and puts in question the usual subordinations depending on age, sex, class, and race. It affects every department of social life, and none more than education. In the old education, which derived its conceptions of discipline from the practice of the military state and minimized the individual, it was taken for granted that the child should yield implicit obedience to the commands of parents and teachers and get the kind of training his elders thought best for him, irrespective of his likes and dislikes or even his special capacities. But once it is recognized that the child has an individuality of his own which cannot be ignored without irretrievable injury to his personality, there comes to be an imperative need for a new kind of education adapted to the requirements of each particular case. With heredity immensely more important than environment, the emphasis must not be laid on discipline and training, but on the spontaneous movements of growth. "The child," says Montessori, "is a body which grows and a soul which develops—these two forms, physiological and psychic, have one eternal font, life itself. We must neither mar nor stifle the mysterious powers which lie within these two forms of growth, but we must await from them the manifestations which we know will succeed one another."[1]

It is not enough, however, for the teacher to await the normal expansion of the child's powers. The wise passivity that comes from a proper respect for natural growth is in no way inconsistent with active help in making this expansion easier and surer. But it is important that whatever help the teacher gives should be of the right kind; and for that the obvious requirement is a definite knowledge of the

[1] It is interesting to compare with this a statement of much the same idea by Froebel. "Education in instruction and training ought to be passive and protective, not directive and interfering. We give young plants and animals both room and time because we know that they will grow properly in accordance with the laws of their nature, and we avoid arbitrary interference with their growth because we know that it would prevent their healthy development; but the young human being is regarded as a piece of wax or a lump of clay which can be moulded into any shape whatever. See how the weed when growing under difficulties shows scarcely a sign of an inner law. Then look at it growing in field or garden and see how perfectly it conforms to law. So children who appear sickly and constrained because their parents have forced upon them a form and calling opposed to their nature in their tender years, might develop in beauty and harmony under natural conditions." (*The Education of Man*, §§ 7, 8.) Froebel is in agreement with Montessori in insisting on the due recognition of individuality. The fundamental difference between them is that whereas she finds the ground of individuality in the Nietzschean life-force, he finds it in the inner law of the child's being as a phase of the divine activity. The consequent difference in practice is enormous.

mind and character of the individual pupil. The old-time pedagogy was a failure, according to Montessori, because it did not understand the principle of studying the pupil before educating him. The new pedagogy is grounded on the study of the individual child.

In insisting on this she is but repeating an idea which has been one of the commonplaces of all enlightened teachers since the time of Rousseau. Where she differs from Rousseau and from most of those who have accepted his view is in the greater exactness of the knowledge she thinks necessary for education. In place of the vague empirical notions with which educators have generally been satisfied, she wants a science of childhood—a pedagogical anthropology comparable with the criminal anthropology of Lombroso or the medical anthropology of De Giovanni. In this conception of the scientific basis of educational work she is following the lead of another great fellow-country-man, the anthropologist Sergi, under whose influence she had come as a student. It was his conviction (and it became Montessori's) that any knowledge that is to be of permanent value for the theory and practice of education must rest on data acquired by the measurement and comparison of large numbers of children. "For several years," he says, in a passage quoted by Montessori as summing up his principles, " I have done battle for an idea concerning the instruction and education of man. . . . My idea was that in order to establish natural, rational methods, it was essential that we make numerous, exact, and rational observations of man as an individual, principally during infancy, which is the age at which the foundations of education and culture must be laid. To measure the head, the height, etc., does not, indeed, mean that we are establishing a system of pedagogy, but it indicates the road which we must follow to arrive at such a system, since if we are to educate an individual we must have a definite and direct knowledge of him."

So far as this is a plea for exact knowledge and the experimental method in education, no objection is likely to be taken to it at this time of day. It is not only the view which would come as a matter of course to one like Montessori, whose training had given acquaintance with the progress made in medicine by a scientific procedure, but a view in keeping with the practical spirit of the age. There is very general agreement that there is no use speculating in general terms about anything that can be put to the test of experience or reduced to a problem in applied mathematics. But if it is implied that only those facts which are measurable have a place in a science of education, as some advocates of the very new science of experimental pedagogy are inclined to declare, it is a different matter. The answer to any such contention may be given in the wise words of Aristotle, that we must be content if we can attain to as great precision in our statements as the subject under consideration allows. Even if it be granted, as indeed it must, that there is considerable scope for the statistical investigation of educational phenomena, it is only a gross exaggeration of the value of the category of number and ignorance of the limited worth of even the highest mathematics when applied to spiritual facts that leads any one to regard as outside the province of science whatever in education defies measurement and calculation. As a matter of fact, most of the significant facts about development of any kind, and more especially about the development of such a complex entity as the human soul, would be ruled out of consideration by this narrow view of science.

It is possible that both Sergi and Montessori would repudiate this doctrinaire position if it were imputed to them. However that be, their attempt at creating a pedagogical anthropology capable of giving such knowledge about the individual child as is necessary for educating him scientifically is vitiated by the undue importance they attach to measurable facts. Implicitly, if not explicitly, they regard those aspects of child life which can be most surely known as those which are most worth knowing. All the really vital facts about education which prove refractory to anthropological methods, and are either not measurable or only imperfectly measurable, are passed over by them with but scanty mention. The facts which can be treated statistically, however unimportant, are regarded as of more account than those not amenable to computation. Thus we find that the greater part of the elaborate treatise which Dr Montessori designates *Pedagogical Anthropology* is occupied with the discussion (for the most part very general) of height and weight, the skull, thorax, pelvis, limbs, skin, etc., of children. From beginning to end the whole concern of the writer is with the child's body, and even with that only in the purely external aspects, which lend themselves most readily to elementary kinds of measurement. There is scarcely a suggestion of interest in mind or soul, such as one might reasonably expect to find in a work professedly dealing with pedagogy, and no attempt is made to present the tolerably exact knowledge about the child as a learner which is beginning to be at the disposal of the educator. It is extraordinary to think that any person can imagine that this kind of information is of real value for the ordinary work of education; and still more extraordinary to learn that the delusion is or was shared by a considerable number of teachers in Italy. Anthropology it may be, though surely of a sorely restricted kind, but not in any proper sense *pedagogical* anthropology.

198

Individuality

One phase of the movement for the establishment of a scientific pedagogy by the anthropological method, however, which might seem to escape the reproach of not bearing directly on education, is the making and keeping of the biographical charts of school-children. In point of fact, the defect of the method is nowhere more apparent than in these attempts to individualize the pupil by a careful record of his most characteristic features. Theoretically the biographical chart should supply the teacher with all the most important facts about each pupil in such form that he can deal with him as an individual. A careful examination of any of the actual charts will show that individuality always eludes the chart-maker.

Let us first consider Montessori's scheme. The items on her main chart are these : A. Name ; age. Name of parents ; mother's age ; father's age ; professions. Hereditary antecedents. Personal antecedents. B. *Anthropological Notes :* Standing stature. Weight. Chest measurement. Sitting stature. Index of height. Index of weight. Head : circumference ; diameter, front to back ; diameter across ; cephalic index. Physical constitution. Muscular condition. Colour of skin. Colour of hair.

This chart of Montessori's is of set purpose simpler than most of the charts advocated and used by other Italian educators. Unlike these, it makes no provision for a physiological or a psychological examination, on the ground that these are too cumbrous to be of real use. The physio-pathological and psychical notes needed to complete the account of the individual child " are got in part from the scholar's records, and in part are determined by the doctor according to the needs of the particular case." The pedagogical methods employed, she points out, being based on the ' spontaneity ' of the child's manifestations, are themselves the technical and rational method of proceeding in the psychic examination of him.

Montessori, it is evident, is not very keen about the ordinary biographical chart, with its mass of detail. But though she greatly reduces the formal cataloguing of the child's attributes by confining it almost entirely to the physical group she neither abandons the practice of chart-making nor gives up the idea of defining individuality by this method or some similar one. At a later point we shall have to return to discuss the implications of her chart, but now for the sake of comparison we pass to the more complete chart of Sergi, intended by him for the observation of school-children at the times of their entry into and their departure from school. The lists of points to be noted in both cases are much alike. Here are those for pupils entering school :

First Table (*Physical Observations*) : Name. Age. Nationality. Parents. Vaccination.

Individuality

Height.   Weight.   Chest measurement.
Muscular power.   General state of health.
Previous illnesses.   Anomalies, deformities.
Circumference of head.   Greatest length of
head.   Greatest breadth of head.   Cephalic
index.   Breadth of face.   Height of face.
Facial index.   Colour and form of hair.
Colour of eyes.   Colour of skin.   Probable
indications.

SECOND TABLE (*Psychological Observations*):
Acuteness of vision, presbyopia or myopia.
Colour vision, normal or defective.   Sensitiveness of hearing.   Sensitiveness of touch.
Intelligence, precocious or backward.   Perception, quick or slow.   Memory, retentive
or weak.   Attention, easily evoked or otherwise.   Speech, quick or slow.   Pronunciation, perfect or imperfect.   Stammering.
Emotional sensibility, obtuse or prone to
imitate.   Conduct and character in the family.
Affection toward parents.   Taciturnity or
loquacity.   Preferences in leisure-time.   Cap-
rices, eccentricities.   Other exceptional facts.

Other and more elaborate charts might be cited.
In a valuable chapter on 'The Biographical History
of the Scholar' in the *Antropologia Pedagogica*,
Montessori gives details of eight, beginning with
that of Seguin (whom she calls the pioneer of the

anthropological method in education), and including a lengthy one recently introduced into the Government reformatories of Italy. But probably the two which have been given will be sufficient for the purpose of the discussion. The question at issue, it will be remembered, is whether, as Sergi and Montessori (among others) assert, it is possible to know a child as a unique individual and to educate him as such with the guidance given by a schedule of characteristics set forth systematically on a biographical chart. Such representative charts as their own should enable us to reach some kind of decision as to the soundness of the contention.

The point, it is to be noted, is not whether the making of a biographical chart or the keeping of a continuous record of each pupil's progress or any other method taken to get exact information about particular children is of value for education in the way of enabling the instruction given to be fitted to the requirements of each case. No one will dispute the contention that the more a teacher knows with precision about his pupils as individuals the better he is likely to teach them; or deny that a teacher with any of the charts before him would most probably have an advantage over one who depended entirely on the casual impressions of the class-room. But surely the high claims made for the biographical chart as indispensable for the establishment of a scientific pedagogy entitle us to expect more than

Individuality

this. If the main result obtained from these anthropological records is only a more intimate view of the individual pupil, they do not seem to differ in any substantial way from the ordinary examination system when used by a competent teacher to guide him in his work. A well-chosen arithmetical test, a theme for composition that tempts the writer to let himself go, a laboratory experiment that calls for personal thought, all reveal individual capacities, and provide the teacher with information about his pupils that is of greater value for his immediate purposes than any general entry in a chart or diary.

To this the answer of the anthropologist might be that the teacher who makes use of examinations to learn about his pupils only deals with individuality at second hand, as it manifests itself in certain detached reactions, but that for his part he presses back to the fundamental attributes of mind and body of which these are derivative products and views them as a whole. That at any rate would be the logical position for him to take. Let us see what it implies.

We may begin with a scrutiny of the characteristics of the individual child which are recorded on the biographical chart. Taking Sergi's table as typical, we note that on the physical side they include the facts of height, weight, head and face measurements, the colour of the hair and the eyes, and similar data, and on the psychical side sensory acuteness, perception, memory, attention, speech habits, emotional sensibility, intelligence, conduct, etc. With one or two exceptions, these are all in a way fundamental facts. But even if it be granted that individuality can be defined in such terms as these, the list of physical and mental units seems a very scanty one from which to construct the whole life of the child. One cannot help asking whether some important qualities have not been omitted. There certainly does not seem to be any notice taken of a great many differences in individual constitution which are vastly more important for education than differences of height or of coloration. No mention, for example, is made of differences in temperament ; in the capacity for improvement and in the relative permanence of the improvement effected ; in the capacity for enduring fatigue ; in the predominant sense-imagery ; in the rapidity of mental operations ; in æsthetic interests ; in literary, mathematical, or other special abilities. And the list of omissions could be extended indefinitely.

The obvious remedy might seem to be an extension of the chart. But to that there is serious objection both on practical and on theoretical grounds. If any considerable number of items be added, the method would break down under the strain of the extra labour involved. It is a simple matter to weigh a child or to measure his skull,

Individuality

but almost any psychological determination (for example, of the preferred sense) requires an elaborate technique and prolonged experimentation. It would take almost as much time to give a tolerably complete account of the mentality of the individual pupil, such as Sergi and Montessori require for the scientific conduct of his education, as it would take to educate him. And even if the teacher could have this complete account of his pupil he would find it beyond his skill to take into account more than a few of the outstanding facts on the extended chart. Montessori practically admits this by reducing her own chart to a list of physical measurements, which are as easily made as they are educationally useless. Had she carried the reasoning that prompted this reduction further, she would have abandoned even the physical measurements as a part of education, and recognized the impossibility of making the education of the individual depend on the prior scheduling of his distinctive qualities.[1]

The theoretical objection to an extension of the chart is even greater than the practical. It is not possible by any addition to the items of the chart to compass individuality, for the simple reason that

[1] To prevent a possible misunderstanding, it may be well to say that my argument is not directed against the acquisition of exact knowledge concerning *children in general* by the experimental method, but against the extraordinary doctrine that there ought to be an exact specification of the psychical characteristics of *every individual child*, as an essential part of the educative process. I believe as strongly in the one as I disbelieve in the other.

individuality is not constituted by a fixed number of unitary attributes. For convenience, we make distinctions that have reference to the subject's behaviour in a particular situation, but as there is an indefinite number of possible situations, no chart can ever adequately define the individual. The most that can be done—and all that the anthropologists have attempted to do with their charts, though they profess to do a great deal more—is to select the more important phases of the individual life for exact characterization. The undoubted utility of this procedure, however, should not be allowed to obscure the fact that to know twenty or forty or any number of individual qualities is not to know the individual.

It would seem, then, from all this that the anthropologist, like the examiner, only knows *about* the individuals whom he undertakes to define. With all his science, or, rather, because of his science, he never succeeds in penetrating to the arcana of individuality. What he really does when he distinguishes one person from another in any special respect is not to individualize him, but to refer him to another and generally to a narrower group. In effect, he displaces a generalization which is too wide and vague to apply with perfect aptness to the individuals to whom it has possible reference, by a more limited generalization which comes closer to the particular case with which he is dealing. He begins, for instance, with the category of 'children,' and then subdivides into children with, say, different kinds of memory or different colours of eyes; but with all his subdividing he never succeeds in getting to the point where his characterization ceases to be a process of grouping and touches the uniqueness of the individual child. There is an interesting illustration of this point in the introductory chapter of Montessori's *Antropologia Pedagogica* (pp. 15, 16), in which the advantages of her method are demonstrated at some length by reference to the educational difference entailed by the poverty of one child and the wealth of another. The assumption she makes is that a system which recognizes these differences is more individual than one which does not. But is it really so? It may be a good thing that the teacher should take both the biological and the social effects of poverty into account in his teaching; but it is surely patent that 'poverty' is quite as much a general idea as 'child,' and that we have not become more individual in our treatment of a child when we have modified the general kind of education assumed to be suitable for all children into another general kind of education assumed to be suitable for poor children.

May we not extend this criticism and say that Montessori's system as a whole, in spite of her insistence on the need of ascertaining the characters of the individual children before educating them, involves the same imposition of a general method on the child which she condemns in other systems ? There is much talk at the beginning of her treatise on *Scientific Pedagogy* about making anthropometrical observations on children, but as the discussion moves on we fail to discover any practical result from this observation. There is scarcely a suggestion of individual behaviour in all the stories about children that illustrate the argument. One somehow gets the impression of them as puppets dancing to the piping of the magician who sways them by her method. Success comes immediately to most of them with a pleasant ease. There do not seem to be any difficulties ; and failures, either temporary or permanent, are decidedly uncommon. This assuredly is not what happens in real life when individuality gets proper scope. If it has happened in the Montessori schools—which is open to doubt— it is the condemnation, not the triumph, of the method.[1]

But, in justice to Dr Montessori, this criticism must be qualified by adding that though individuality has eluded her scientific method and does not figure very prominently in her own statement of the

[1] In this connexion it may be worth while to quote a passage from a trenchant criticism of the Montessori method by Professor J. A. Green (*Journal of Experimental Pedagogy*, March 1913, p. 48): "As a scientific treatise, the Montessori book seems to me thoroughly shallow and disappointing, because it gives no account of the failures or of the difficulties of the system. It is the Swiss Family Robinson of educational literature. . . . Some children learn to read and write. . . . We

Individuality

results of her work, there is actually a greater place for it in her educational scheme than in the ordinary schools. The reason for this is to be found in the fact to which attention has already been called: that while professing adherence to Sergi's doctrine of starting with a knowledge of individual characters and making the methods of education conform to this, she virtually abandons it with respect to mental characters. Instead of saying, "This is the kind of mind the child has, and therefore he should be educated in this particular way," she leaves him free to show by his response to his environment what kind of mind he has and to find for himself the means of education; and so she has accomplished indirectly what she failed to accomplish directly. She invented her system of didactic apparatus to meet a generic need of child nature, but instead of forcing it upon her pupils because it would be suitable for them as children, she allowed each pupil to use it in the way that seemed good to him, and so gave individuality the chance to assert itself. Thus she discovered, without clearly appreciating the significance of her discovery, that the right way

are not told whether all did, or whether the acquirement was of any use to them, or whether they learned equally quickly, or whether they lost the art subsequently. That some or all of these things did happen I have no doubt. . . . If you would take the trouble to compare this sort of thing with any ordinary laboratory record of the study of animal behaviour, shall we say, you would realize the difference between an account of scientific procedure and the collection of pretty stories which illuminate Madame Montessori's book."

to encourage the inner development of the child is not by a scheme of education based on the teacher's knowledge of his individuality—though that may be helpful enough so long as the teacher does not restrict the child by a possibly wrong conception of his character—but by leaving him free and providing occasion for the exercise of capacities without which individuality cannot come to its full perfection.

Not only so, but she has shown that the grouping of children for purposes of instruction in the early years of life (and, it may be, at a more advanced age) is not incompatible with the mental and moral well-being of each individual child. Her demonstration, it is true, only applies to her own system, but there is no reason in the nature of either teaching or learning for supposing that its validity is thus confined. In any system—in Montessori's as much as any other—what is taught is always of general import. However much the teacher adapt instruction to the child, he must always adapt it to the child in general or to some type of child. He can never individualize it. True mental appropriation, on the other hand, is always a matter for the child himself and cannot be anything else than individual. If, therefore, Montessori has succeeded by means of her method in calling forth a higher degree of creative action in the process of learning, and made it less easy for the child to echo the experiences and ideas of others, her discovery has value for all educators.

CHAPTER X

FREEDOM

DR MONTESSORI'S discussion of individuality is vitiated by her failure to realize that human individuality is a social, not a biological fact. No doubt the factor of inheritance enters into it, but the inherited characters peculiar to the individual only get marshalled into an individuality in becoming transformed through education into the attributes of a social being. This is generally overlooked by those who, like Montessori, undertake the advocacy of the rights of any section of humanity, because the consciousness of individuality is a revolutionary product which emerges in the protest of the ever-advancing spirit of man against the restrictions imposed by outgrown institutions. In the confusion of the conflict, it seems to the protestant that he is vindicating the inherent rights of the individual not merely against particular forms of social life, but against society itself. As a matter of fact, the rights that are claimed are not in any sense independent of society. They are anticipations of a higher social order which have grown out of the existing order of things, and they bear on them the stamp of their time. Instead of being a fixed entity, unaffected by society, as the biological analogy appears to suggest, the human individual draws the substance of his being from the ideals of his age.

In Montessori's case the antagonism between man and society assumes a form which makes any reconciliation of the opposing interests peculiarly difficult to conceive. If, as she thinks, the individual person is a manifestation of the mysterious (non-rational ?) life-force, the essence of individuality is spontaneity, impulse, self-assertion. If not anti-social, it is at least non-social. For force translated into terms of human mentality becomes will, and in mere will there is no potency of social relationships of any kind. The will to live that each man borrows from the great world-force is a striving to live his own life; and any restriction, whether natural or social, that prevents him doing so is an infringement of his very nature as a man. Yet is not society on any view of its constitution restrictive? "Civilized life," as Montessori says, "is made by renunciation of the life of nature." [1] It involves the constant checking of individual impulses, the imposition of 'bonds.' How then can there be any place for individuality in this society which "is made up solely of renunciations and restraints" ? [2]

---

[1] *The Montessori Method*, p. 153.
[2] *Ibid.*, p. 152.

Freedom

The fact is that on Montessori's premises it is impossible to get a coherent view of the relations of the individual and society, of the inner impulse and the outer law. But being more concerned about practice than theory, she is not disturbed by the fundamental inconsistencies of her unconscious philosophy. Limiting her attention to her educational work, she meets the encroachments of social life on the individuality of the child with a demand for freedom—by which she means the absence of interference with the processes of growth. " We cannot know the consequences of suffocating a *spontaneous action* at the time when the child is just beginning to be active: perhaps we suffocate *life itself.* Humanity shows itself in all its intellectual splendour during this tender age, as the sun shows itself at the dawn, and the flower at the first unfolding of the petals; and we must *respect* religiously, reverently, these first indications of individuality. If any educational act is to be efficacious, it will be only that which tends to *help* toward the complete unfolding of this life. To be thus helpful it is necessary rigorously to avoid *the arrest of spontaneous movements and the imposition of arbitrary tasks.*" Then quite illogically she adds : " It is of course understood that here we do not speak of useless or dangerous acts, for these must be *suppressed, destroyed.*" [1]

---

[1] *The Montessori Method*, pp. 87, 88.

From Locke to Montessori

The reason for the qualification is obvious enough. It is easy to talk about freedom in the abstract and to condemn all restrictions that prevent spontaneity of action. But in the concrete that means letting the child do what he likes, and that kind of liberty is not possible in Montessori's or any other school. For practical purposes, therefore, she has to find a position midway between the absolute freedom required by her theory of individuality and the renunciations and restraints which in her view are characteristic of the social relationships; and she does so by tacitly abandoning the non-social kind of freedom and substituting for it a modified form of social freedom. Her first attempt at the definition of this latter kind of freedom is made by stipulating that the child shall be allowed, and even encouraged, to act without the least restriction, so long as his actions do not interfere with the like freedom on the part of others. " The liberty of a child," she says, "should have as its *limit* the collective interest: as its *form*, what we universally consider good breeding. We must, therefore, check in the child whatever offends or annoys others, or whatever tends toward rough or ill-bred acts."

The sentiment is quite unimpeachable, but it comes strangely from Montessori. By what right does she impose limits of any kind on freedom? According to her own hypothesis, the life-force which impels the child to spontaneous action is

Freedom

essentially good in its manifestations. Is there any reason for making an exception in despite of quarrelling, fighting, and similar anti-social actions, apart from conventions which she herself cannot consistently recognize? Such an exception surely lays her open to the charge of crushing out innate tendencies of the child which there is some reason to think may be as necessary for the complete development of the individual mind and character as the others which society permits. This is precisely the charge she brings against the ordinary school. But even if it be granted that the child's spontaneous actions ought to be ruthlessly repressed when they are contrary to social well-being, what criterion is to be used in discriminating between those actions which are to be permitted and those which are not? Montessori's test is the accepted standards of good breeding. The child must not merely refrain from positively injurious acts, but from those which offend his elders. In speaking about discipline, Montessori bewails the fact that her first teachers misunderstood what she meant by freedom and allowed the children to do what they pleased. "I saw children with their feet on the tables or with their fingers in their noses, and no intervention was made to correct them. I saw others push their companions, and I saw dawn in the faces of these an expression of violence; and not the slightest attention on the part of the teacher. Then I had to

215

intervene to show with what absolute rigour it is necessary to hinder, and little by little suppress, all those things which we must not do." But why, on her own idea of freedom, should not the children put their feet on the tables or their fingers in their noses ? If the only objection is that these acts offend conventional adults, then the whole case for free development is given away. There is not the slightest diffcrence in principle between these restrictions and those of ordinary parents and teachers. The insistence on silence and immobility in the class-room which Montessori condemns so vigorously is capable of justification on the same grounds. She may be right in her practical maxims, but the reason she gives for them is quite wrong.

The attempt to define freedom as doing what one pleases so long as there is no interference with the pleasure of others thus breaks down. But the identification of freedom with independence, by which, as we have seen,[1] Montessori tries to give her *laissez-faire* doctrine a positive content, seems to present a view of social freedom that is not open to the same condemnation. The argument is this. The person who is served by another is limited by his dependence, and any limitation is incompatible with freedom; consequently a training in self-help, which will remove this

[1] Ch. vii. p. 142.

limitation, is an essential part of the education for freedom.

The underlying assumption that freedom means the absence of limitation is plainly inconsistent with Montessori's general conception of liberty under social conditions; but as it is consistent, for that very reason, with her doctrine of the individual as deriving his life from the world-force, there is no need to dwell upon that. The real difficulty is in the implication of the assumption. In a social world where we all constantly depend for the satisfaction of the most elementary needs of life on the labours of a vast number of our fellows it is absurd to speak of freedom as consisting in the absence of dependence. Even in a savage tribe where the economic organization is only rudimentary the individual never lives entirely by his own efforts: much less, therefore, is independence conceivable in a society like ours, with the division of labour indefinitely extended. Montessori would of course disclaim the interpretation of her principles which leads to this *reductio ad absurdum*. But it is the logical outcome of a consistent individualism, and there is no escape from it except into the vagueness and confusion of thought that characterizes her first definition of freedom. Let us suppose that she qualifies her doctrine by the admission that society in any form must be based on some measure of dependence, and that it is only the dependence which removes the necessity for the exercise of personal powers that is bad. We may agree with her practical deductions from this view: that the man whose talents are never called forth because he does not need to work for his bread and the child who is dressed and fed by others when he might be attending to himself are both harmfully dependent on others and are likely to suffer in their own development in consequence of it. But as soon as we ask for a principle by which to discern bad forms of dependence from good, we discover the practical barrenness of Montessori's conception of freedom. The fact is that once she lets go the idea that all dependence is bad, she has no means of distinguishing good from bad. Her conception of freedom is fundamentally negative, and she can only give it an appearance of being positive by a more or less arbitrary specification of acts which she says are done in independence and freedom. The elaborate insistence on the necessity for free development through independent activity reduces itself in practice to the vague precept that as far as possible children should learn " to walk without assistance, to run, to go up and down stairs, to lift up fallen objects, to dress and undress themselves, to bathe themselves, to speak distinctly, and to express their own needs clearly." [1] Apart from the fact that no attempt is made to distinguish legitimate from illegitimate help, there is

[1] *The Montessori Method*, p. 97.

nothing to object to in this. It is certainly not an epoch-making discovery. Rousseau said it all a hundred and fifty years ago,[1] and many intelligent mothers have found it out for themselves. In any case it does not make much difference to the children. They contrive to learn all these things whatever happens.

Enough has been said of the inconsistencies of Montessori's conceptions of freedom to dispose of her claim to be the first to make freedom an effective pedagogical principle. But it would be a mistake to insist so much on the imperfections of her statement of the case as to obscure the fact that she has obtained a very considerable success in practice in spite of her defective theory. All the evidence available seems to show that she has succeeded in giving the children in her schools a real freedom, and that the results of her work, so far as they can be judged on a short view, are eminently satisfactory in this respect. The scholars are not put under any constraint, but they devote themselves to their

[1] In view of Montessori's mistaken disparagement of Rousseau's advocacy of freedom in education (*The Montessori Method*, p. 15), it is necessary to say that there is nothing she has said on the subject which has not been as well said by Rousseau. The remarkable identity of their views can only be properly appreciated by a careful reading of the first three books of the *Emile*, but the following passage may serve to illustrate it: "Le seul qui fait sa volonté est celui qui n'a pas besoin, pour la faire, de mettre les bras d'un autre au bout des siens: d'où il suit que le premier de tous biens n'est pas l'autorité mais la liberté. L'homme vraiment libre ne veut que ce qu'il peut, et fait ce qu'il lui plaît." (*Emile*, ii. 30.)

tasks with assiduity and good-will. There is a complete absence of the ordinary forms of discipline —there are no commands or threats, no rewards or punishments—yet there is no serious misbehaviour, and even petty misdemeanours are rare. The very lack of external regulations has the effect of calling an unexpected power of self-direction into play.

How are these results to be explained? Some of the critics of the system account for them by saying that the scholars in the Children's Houses in Italy belong for the most part to the poorest and worst-fed section of the population and that their low vitality makes them more amenable to a quiet, unobtrusive discipline than the well-to-do children of a more energetic nation would be. The explanation has a certain plausibility, but it does not go very far. As a matter of fact, badly nurtured children are not generally more easily controlled than others. Bad health and low vitality are as likely to make children restless and capricious as tame and spiritless. In any case it is not quite true to say that the Montessori system has only worked well in poor neighbourhoods. Its greatest triumphs have been there because of the greater need for good educational methods. But considerable success has been achieved by it among better-class children in Italy as well as in America. So far as can be judged from the small number of

Freedom

of the children to do what they see others doing. They observe the performance of certain actions, and even without a proper understanding of their significance they are eager to follow the example set and to repeat the actions for themselves. This has the semblance of freedom, but whether it is real freedom is another question All depends on what it is that the children are required to imitate and how long the practice of unintelligent imitation goes on. In the early years of life, however, the method of imitation is for most purposes superior to any method that is predominantly verbal and mandatory; for the children have at least the stimulus to learning that comes from the sense of personal effort and are not retarded in their development by the consciousness of hampered activities.

The case that is least open to criticism is that in which children learn from each other. The child sees his little playmates marching round, and he falls into line and marches with them. He sees some older boy or girl handling the sandpaper letters and finally breaking spontaneously into literary expression; he becomes eager to do the same, and, imitating all the time, perseveres in his endeavour until he also has mastery of the art of writing. The value of this mutual instruction is scarcely to be doubted; no form of education is so free from factitious adult devices. The only point that provokes question is whether Montessori does not underrate the part played by adult models and attach undue importance to the spontaneous invention of modes of expression by the children. Her theory would seem to be that until they actually begin to write or to dance for themselves (to take two actual examples) no attempt should be made to teach them how to do these things. But here she overlooks the fact that an art can only be created once *ab origine* in any school, and thereafter the spontaneity of discovery prompted by imitation must necessarily be on a lower level of achievement. Surely it would be better to recognize this frankly and not await the chance advent of a more than average pupil to set the sequence of imitated actions in progress? Why should the beginning not be made by the teacher?

That would mean that the children instead of imitating one another would imitate the teacher; and the doubt immediately suggests itself whether this is consistent with the principle of educational freedom as enunciated by Montessori. Let us consider a particular case recorded by an American observer.[1] On one occasion when she was present at the lunch hour in one of the Children's Houses in Rome she noticed that one little boy could not tuck his napkin under his chin and waited to see what would happen. After wrestling with the napkin for some time, the boy brought it to the

[1] Fisher, *A Montessori Mother*, pp. 25–29.

teacher. "So sure was I of what her action would be," says the writer, "that I fairly felt my own hands follow hers in the familiar motions of tucking the napkin under a child's round chin." Instead of doing that, "she held it up in her hands, showed the child how to take hold of a larger part of the corner than he had been grasping, and illustrating on herself gave him an object-lesson." But even then he failed to accomplish the task. The teacher took the napkin once more and went through all the movements quite slowly, and this time all went well. The lady who records the incident is so struck with the fact that the teacher did not follow the ordinary plan of tucking in the child's napkin for him that she fails to see that showing a child how to do a thing like this may involve doing all the child's trying and thinking for him and be as much contrary to the principle of independence as the physical help. What would Montessori have done in these circumstances? Her conception of independence is so vague that it is impossible to say. There is undoubtedly a considerable amount of 'showing' in the Children's Houses, not merely in such simple matters as the carrying of a tureen or the setting of a table, but in more important ones. Her prescription for securing obedience, as we have seen, is to *show* the children how to obey. That presumably means in most cases that the teacher sets an example for the pupils to imitate.

But the situation is by no means free from difficulty, in view of her insistence on the necessity for freedom in learning. " In consideration of the system of liberty which I proposed," she says, when speaking of plastic work in clay, " I did not like to make the children *copy* anything." That would seem to apply equally to learning to use a napkin. But what is the alternative ? Evidently that children are only to be allowed to learn what they originate or discover for themselves. That is the conclusion to be drawn from Montessori's ordinary statement of her position, and in some cases at any rate she does not shrink from it. The scholars in the first Children's Houses did not draw or sing or recite poetry, seemingly because it would involve an amount of direction on the teacher's part inconsistent with the possibilities of individual discovery. Rather than have them shown these simple arts at the expense of what she regards as their liberty, she deprives them of the extraordinary pleasure and stimulus which experience shows they afford to young learners. When adherence to a general principle forces one to an extreme position like this, it is time for a revision of the premises of the argument which led to it. The question that must ultimately be raised is whether it is possible for children to learn anything at all without imitating those who are their superiors in wisdom and experience ; and if so whether dependence on others is the

Freedom

evil condition which Montessori seems to consider it. That question can only be answered by modifying the conception of freedom which is the starting-point of the system, so as to recognize a dependence which is not servile, and a learning from others which is not destructive of personal effort and individuality.

CHAPTER XI

THE EDUCATION OF THE SENSES

THE combination of the doctrine of freedom with a scheme of sense-training in the Montessori system appears at first sight to be a matter of accident that is only to be explained by the idiosyncrasy of Montessori's thought. But a brief consideration of the practical developments of modern individualism, especially in the spheres of politics and education, will show that the connexion is by no means a haphazard one. We have only to think of Montessori's predecessors to see with what constancy the two lines of thought make their appearance together. And if we go beyond the history of education to the history of philosophy the conjunction is even more striking. Again and again since the time of Locke we find sensationalism associated with a noble passion for freedom and playing a worthy part in the cause of progress. The reason is fairly obvious. Sensation is the most intimate and personal phase of mind, the prominent fact in our thought whenever we make direct, first-hand acquaintance with the physical world, our guarantee to ourselves that our knowledge is our own. Consequently the one-sided emphasis on the sensory elements which is characteristic of the sensationalist philosophy forces attention upon what is individual in experience as opposed to the dictates of external authority. There is implicit in it the impulse to revolt against the truth which has not proved itself truth for the individual and the law which he has not accepted as his law. From that negation to the assertion of a positive right to freedom is but a short step.[1]

Montessori, it is true, is not a sensationalist in her metaphysics. Her ultimate explanation of man and the universe is given in terms of force or will rather than of sensation. But the difference in effect is unimportant. For the pragmatic accentuation of will in theory readily passes into sensationalism in practice; and in any case the psychology which has inspired her educational methods is sensationalist to the core.

The basis of that psychology is the vague materialistic view of mind which is part of the medical tradition resulting from the habit of approaching mind through body and thinking of the psychical as an outgrowth from the physiological. In her case it is redeemed from some of its crudeness by the recognition that medical treatment is not

[1] For a general statement of the relation of sensationalism and the principle of freedom see Dewey, *The Influence of Darwin on Philosophy, and other Essays*, pp. 290–295.

always sufficient where mind is concerned and that sometimes the relation must be reversed and education take the place of medicine by making mind help body. That, however, does not alter the fundamental character of her working conception of mind. In substance, the view she holds is one somewhat like the three-level theory made familiar to English thinkers by Dr Hughlings Jackson and found of service in the diagnosis of epileptic and similar cases.[1] She thinks of mind as beginning in purely physiological processes, developing into sensory-motor activities, and finally attaining the higher forms of mentality, each successive stage differing from its predecessor in character.

This conception of mind as a series of detached functions received further exaggeration on the sensory side from her study of experimental psychology for educational purposes. In the laboratory the experimenter is forced by the conditions of his work to deal with sensory discrimination and the other phenomena of mind in an artificial detachment. It is not memory with its concrete fullness of detail with which he concerns himself, but such simple forms of memory as the memory of nonsense syllables from which the complications of the higher mental processes have been largely excluded. So in the sphere of the senses (which seem to have been the main subject of Montessori's study) it is not the

[1] *Cf.* M'Dougall, *Physiological Psychology*, chaps. iii.–iv.

actual use of the sense organs with their bewildering interrelations with mental process as a whole that is dealt with, but the sense activities in their most abstract and elementary forms. In this the experimental psychologist is following the method of all scientific workers, and the conclusions he draws are quite valid within their limits. The danger is that when he comes to education and has to deal with the senses, not in the detachment proper to psychology, but as elements in the mental life of a potentially rational being, he may be tempted to regard the abstract units of laboratory practice as the actual starting-point of sensory experience and give what are only fragments of mind a value greater than their due. That seems to be what Montessori has done in her insistence on an elaborate scheme of sense-training.

Whether that be so or not, it is the view of mind formed under the conjoint influences of her professional studies as a doctor and her work in the psychological laboratory that underlies her educational methods, and we cannot discuss their wisdom or unwisdom profitably until we have considered the conception of the child mind which she deduces from it for guidance in the work of the school.

Our aim in education, she says, is twofold, biological and social. From the biological side we wish to help the natural development of the

individual; from the social standpoint it is our aim
to prepare the individual for his environment.
These two phases of education are always inter-
woven, but one or other is predominant according
to the age of the child. In early childhood it is the
former. The period of life between the ages of three
and seven is a period of rapid physical development. It is the time for the formation of the sense
activities as related to the intellect. The stimuli,
and not yet the reasons of things, attract the child's
attention. Consequently this is the time when we
should methodically direct the sense stimuli, in
such fashion that the sensations which he receives
shall develop in a rational way. This sense-training
will prepare the ordered foundation upon which
he may build up a clear and strong mentality.
Besides all this, it is possible while educating
the senses to discover and eventually to correct
their defects. This education, therefore, is physiological and prepares directly for intellectual education by perfecting the organs of sense and the
nerve paths of projection and sensation. The
other part of education, the adaptation of the
individual to his environment, is involved indirectly; for the method prepares the child to be
an observer, and so fits him for a civilization that
is based on observation.[1]

[1] *The Montessori Method*, pp. 215–217. By way of commentary on
the conception of the child mind here implied, and incidentally to

The Education of the Senses

Montessori, it will be seen, regards the years from three to seven as predominantly the formative period of the sense activities and thinks that the child's education at this time of life should be largely occupied with the training of the senses. Before we can either agree or disagree with her we must be clear as to what is meant by sense activity. (*a*) Does it mean the act of discriminating between the various stimuli that give rise to sensations of weight, colour, sound, heat, etc., without reference to meaning—the mere touching, hearing, seeing, feeling? This is presumably what takes place when an infant turns his eyes to the light that flickers on the wall or when a child knows a colour so directly that he can pair it with its like without consideration of name or conscious effort at distinction. A negative instance that helps to make this physiological meaning of sense activity comprehensible is the case of those children whom Itard found not to be deaf, though unable to hear because the ear had never been adequately used. (*b*) Or does it mean the

emphasize the fact that Montessori's psychology is a doctor's psychology, I give the quotation from the annual report for 1909 of the Chief Medical Officer of the Board of Education which Mr Holmes uses in his pamphlet to illustrate Montessori's view: "The mentally defective child is abnormal in that his brain remains in the childlike condition of being able to do little more than receive sensory impressions by objective means. He can form ideas of things and movements, but he fails to combine and contrast, to associate and to judge. Symbolical concepts do not come to him, and he is unable to draw analogies."

appreciation of sensory differences that finds expression in language—that is shown, for example, by recognizing particular colours, like red or blue, when the name is mentioned, or by the ability to say after touching that one surface is rough and another smooth? (*c*) Or, again, does it mean a process of judgment and reasoning with regard to sense-perceived objects, dependent on accurate discrimination? This, it will be remembered, is what Rousseau takes it to mean. According to him, the boy who finds his way about in the dark by means of touch, or who decides at sight whether a plank is long enough to stretch across a brook, has well-trained senses. "To exercise the senses," he says, " is not only to make use of them: it involves learning to judge accurately by their means." [1]

Now it is essential for the understanding of Montessori's position to keep in mind that when she speaks of the sense activity that is characteristic of children from three to seven she almost expressly excludes the last of these ideas. The child's attention at this age, she affirms, " is attracted to the environment under the form of passive curiosity. The stimuli, and not yet the reasons for things, attract his attention." [2] That is to say, the sensations he experiences when he hears, sees, and touches are what mainly occupy his mind. In the absence of

---

[1] *Emile*, ii. p. 97.
[2] *The Montessori Method*, p. 216.

The Education of the Senses

the higher mental activity, he makes little or no attempt to interpret the sensory data in rational terms. They exist for him as complete facts in themselves. He appreciates the differences between them and acts upon them, even, it may be, names them; but that is nearly all. Comparisons and judgments of the adult type are not involved, and considerations of use, whether personal or social, are generally remote.

It follows from this that the training of the senses in early childhood takes two forms, corresponding to the first and second ideas of sense activity. The more fundamental of the two is concerned with the simple act of discriminating, which necessarily, according to Montessori, precedes all the more complex activities of sense. This is the real sense education, and it is prominent in all the sense exercises of her didactic system. The primary aim in every case is not knowledge about the sensations or the achievement of specific tasks on the sensory level, but the acquisition of a fineness of differential perception which will enable the trained sense to do its proper work at a later age as an instrument of the developed mind. The second form of training is concerned with the association of sensation and name. It is here that Seguin's three steps come in. The child is told the name of the sensory object, learns to recognize the object corresponding to name, and becomes able to remember the object when he hears the name.[1]

The conception of sense function that underlies Montessori's didactic system has been adversely criticized on the ground that it involves the idea of a formal training of the senses, but it is doubtful whether the criticism is sound. Montessori certainly thinks that the sense organs when once trained will be able to do their work under all varieties of circumstances; and she insists on the necessity for a general training of the senses as a preparation for tasks so different as those of a cook and a doctor.[2] But apart altogether from the question of the possibility of a transfer of sensory capacity, on which there is still need for experiment, it is by no means certain that there is any transfer of capacity in the present case at all. If, as Montessori thinks, the result of the training is to establish definite physiological habits, these might

[1] See ch. vii. p. 159.

[2] Montessori is not perfectly consistent in her remarks on this point. Once or twice she lapses into statements which imply the need for a specific training of the senses for the work of adult life. Thus : "We ask the cook to buy only 'fresh fish.' She understands the idea, and tries to follow it in her marketing, but if she has not been trained to recognize through sight and smell the signs which indicate freshness in the fish she will not know how to follow the order we have given her." (*The Montessori Method*, p. 218.) This really stultifies the whole didactic system, for there is not a single exercise in Montessori's scheme which has such a direct bearing on future occupations as this. The girl who is going to be a cook gets her sight trained by fitting insets into frames and matching colours, not by looking at fish.

The Education of the Senses

conceivably be called into play under the most diverse conditions without themselves undergoing any change. The processes established in connexion with the ear through the distinguishing of musical sounds or miscellaneous noises, for example, may have so much in common with those necessary for the accurate discrimination of heart sounds that some form of ear-training in childhood may be indispensable for the future doctor. At any rate, it would be an act of unwarrantable dogmatism to deny the possibility on the general ground that all education must be perfectly specific in character. The doctrine of the uselessness of formal training is as yet too vague and too insecurely founded to be turned into such a comprehensive dogma.

The real objection to Montessori's system of sense-training is that it is based on a wrong notion of the mental characteristics of the young child. Misled by physiological analogies and by the practice of the psychological laboratory, Montessori assumes that the senses as the simplest elements of mind come to an early perfection in individual development, and interprets the child mind as though it were dominated by its sensory experiences. She is led by this to think of the child from three to seven as essentially passive, absorbed in sense stimuli without any concern about their meaning, largely if not wholly lacking in what she vaguely terms the

237

higher mental activities. This is the child for whom her method is devised, and the only one for whom it is suitable. But is there such a child? It is indeed difficult to understand how any person not completely blinded by doctrinaire prejudices could confuse this figment of the scientific imagination with a flesh-and-blood person. It only needs the sympathetic study of a five-year-old boy or girl of ordinary intelligence to show that both in what it includes and in what it omits this is an entirely erroneous account of the child.

Let us consider, to begin with, the characteristics attributed to him (or her). He finds satisfaction in sensations for their own sake, we are told, and does not trouble about the reasons for them. " A day with any normal child will give ample evidence of the delight that children take in purely formal exercises," writes Professor H. W. Holmes. "The sheer fascination of tucking a card under the edge of a rug will keep a baby happy until any ordinary supply of cards is exhausted; and the wholly sensory appeal of throwing stones into the water gives satisfaction enough to absorb for a long time the attention of older children—to say nothing of grown-ups." [1] The truth in this is that in early life there is an unmistakable sense hunger which occasionally makes a child take pleasure in the use of his senses in what an adult would regard as

[1] Introduction to *The Montessori Method*, p. xxxiii.

The Education of the Senses

unmeaning ways. The error in it—and it is a serious error—is to regard it as a distinctive feature of mental life from three to seven. In point of fact, as Professor Holmes's examples indicate, it is not peculiar to these years. So far as it is characteristic of the child at all, it is in babyhood or in the second year. Later it is only an incident which grows less common with advancing years, but does not wholly disappear even in grown-up people. After two the interest of the child is mainly directed outward to the things that cause the sensations, and even from that early time they are not mere things to be taken for granted by him. So far from not concerning himself with the reasons for them, he is busy by three inquiring industriously ' What ? ' ' Why ? ' ' How ? ' or (most frequently of all) asking whether a thing is what he thinks it is. It is passing strange to hear a child of three or four described as mentally passive.

But, it may be said, even if Montessori has exaggerated the detachment of sense activity from personal interest and the absorption of the child in his sensations, there are still substantial grounds for regarding early childhood as the period of life in which the senses are predominant in mind, and that is sufficient justification for special attention being paid to the education of the senses then. This contention is difficult to discuss, because it is not clear what is meant by the predominance of the senses. If what is meant is that sense activity is the outstanding fact during these years, the only thing to be said is that that is not true. The unsophisticated observer will note a great many facts about childhood that are at least as fundamental as sense activity, which have been completely ignored in Montessori's characterization of the child. There is the imagination, showing itself in the desire to hear stories and to act them out in the serious make-believe of play. There is curiosity, not passive, as Montessori thinks it, but even from the beginning a quest for the meanings and values of things. There is the interest in words, containing in it the promise and the potency of generalization. The senses, of course, count for much, as indeed they do all through life, but assuredly not the sensations. The child is constantly concerned with concrete sense-given facts, but, with the exceptions already mentioned, it is not because they are sense-given. Put such facts before him, and his mind immediately goes to work to escape from them: imagination, curiosity, nomination are brought in to transform the sense presentations and subordinate them to the interests of a being who even at this age is not confined to the world of the senses.[1]

---

[1] By way of illustration a most illuminating comment on Montessori's apparatus by Professor J. A. Green may be given : "Watch a small child with the apparatus she provides—take the cylinder insets as examples. He masters the secret in a very short time, and then he turns the cylinders into soldiers, and his big brother of five suggests

The Education of the Senses

It is possible that the case for sense-training may be argued on the more restricted ground that whatever other capacities of mind may be active in early childhood, the senses at any rate are at their formative or nascent period, and need culture if they are to attain to their maximum development in later life. Apart from the recognition of other capacities, this is how Montessori herself sometimes states the case.

Various questions are raised by this contention. The first is whether the child from three to seven is really at the nascent period of the senses. By the nascent period of an organ is meant the time of life when it is developing most rapidly and is most susceptible to educative influences. Can it be said that the senses of a child of five or six are at this stage? In spite of the large amount of work which has been done on the psychology of the senses, it is scarcely possible to answer this with any certainty. But if trust be put in one's experience of children, one would be inclined to doubt whether Montessori has not antedated the maximum activity of the senses by three or four years at least.[1] It is worthy

the holes shall be trenches and the block of wood a fort. Now the whole business is spiritualized. It is a human thing now which we can all watch with interest. But of this kind of escape from the prison-house of didactic materials there is never a word." (*Journal of Experimental Pedagogy*, March 1913, p. 50.)

[1] Touch is perhaps an exception. There is no doubt that Montessori has done real service to education by showing the great value of tactile experiences in early childhood. The success of her method of teaching writing, for example, is to be referred to the use she makes of touch.

of note that Rousseau, whose psychological intuitions were extraordinarily sure, regarded the whole period from infancy till the age of twelve as the time for sense-training. That perhaps goes to the other extreme and underrates the development of the boy of twelve, but it accords better with the general impression that the senses are most satisfactorily trained about nine or ten.

The second question is whether it is worth training the senses specifically at all. When we find, for example, that the æsthesiometric data show an inverse correlation with general intelligence (children and savages appearing to have a more acute tactile sensibility than educated adults),[1] we begin to suspect that Montessori's didactic system is a house built on sand. The whole question, however, is an open one. " Some writers are convinced that keen discrimination is a prerequisite to keen intelligence, while others are equally convinced that intelligence is essentially conditioned by ' higher processes,' and only remotely by sensory capacity." We may leave the matter at that, with the note of doubt. Apart from the question of the relation between sense-training and intelligence, there is the important consideration that, as Professor Whipple points out, the normal capacity of all the senses is many times in excess of the actual demands of life.

[1] *Cf.* Burt, *Experimental Tests of General Intelligence*, in *The British Journal of Psychology*, iii. p. 119.

The Education of the Senses

"The very fact of the existence of this surplus capacity seems to negative at the outset the notion that sensory capacity can be a conditioning factor in intelligence," [1] and stultifies any system of sense-training like Montessori's. Obviously there is no purpose to be served by training the senses if they are already more than sufficient for the requirements of life. Montessori, however, would not admit that they are sufficient. She asserts that all sorts and conditions of people, from cooks to doctors, fail in their business because their senses are incompetent. "One day," she says, "I heard a surgeon giving to a number of poor mothers a lesson on the first deformities noticeable in little children from the disease of rickets. The mothers understood the idea, but they did not know how to recognize these first signs of deformity, because they were lacking in the sensory education through which they might discriminate between signs deviating only slightly from the normal." [2] Here Montessori is surely finding the defect where she wants to find it. There is nothing in such a case to indicate that these women had not perfectly good eyesight for objects within the range of their knowledge. If they could not make proper use of their eyes, it was probably their intelligence that was at fault rather than their senses.

[1] Whipple, *Manual of Mental and Physical Tests*, p. 130, quoted in the introduction to *The Montessori Method*.

[2] *The Montessori Method*, p. 220.

From Locke to Montessori

This leads up to the third question, whether the senses do not get all the training they need incidentally to the cultivation of the general intelligence. Montessori's assumption throughout her exposition of the didactic system is that the senses need to be trained in detachment from the higher mental processes. There does not seem to be any reason to think, however, that a person of ordinary capacity who has not received a special training of this kind is in any way handicapped by the lack of it. His touch is not so sensitive as a blind man's; his hearing is not so effective in appreciating shades of difference in musical sounds as that of a musician; his eye does not distinguish colours so well as that of an artist. But it would take more than the few hypothetical illustrations of doubtful interpretation given by Montessori to disprove the general efficiency of his senses, or to justify the establishment of courses of general sensory training for his benefit. Even an untrained child of four, if brought up in a good home, rarely makes a mistake in interpreting the multitude of sounds in his neighbourhood, and when blindfolded can name at once every common article put into his hands. What has he or any one else to gain by formal exercises which for the most part can only give him an abstract acquaintance with sensory qualities that he will come to know well enough in any case as his experience widens?

CHAPTER XII

THE OMISSION OF THE HUMANISTIC
SUBJECTS

ONE of the most unsatisfactory features of the Montessori system is the complete absence of all the subjects which make a direct æsthetic and moral appeal to the child. The pupils in the Children's Houses do not recite poetry or sing songs or dance. Stories are never told to them and no opportunity is given for dramatic action. They colour with brush and crayon, but they never draw or model in clay. They get no religious teaching. Their whole time seems to be spent on the beggarly level of the senses. It is little wonder that some of Montessori's admirers are eager to broaden out her curriculum by the eclectic device of combining it with the Froebelian or some other system which recognizes more adequately the humanity of the pupils.

The shortcomings of her scheme in this respect were pointed out to Montessori by Mr Holmes. Her answer to the criticism was that the omission of these subjects was due to the fact that her system was still in its infancy and that in course of time they

245

would all be brought in. Drawing, dancing, modelling, and every kind of artistic expression, she assured him, were not only included, but had the same important part in her programme as they have in ordinary life; and in confirmation of this she referred to the fact that in one of her schools the children had spontaneously invented dances of their own, and had begun of themselves to draw in primitive fashion. But, adds Mr Holmes significantly, "having recently [May 1912] revisited Rome, I find that the curriculum in the Montessori schools has been in no respect widened since my former visit." [1]

As a matter of fact, Montessori's failure to do justice to the humanistic subjects is not, as her observations to Mr Holmes would seem to imply, a mere accident which is capable of being repaired by the extension of her system. It is deeply rooted both in her temperament and in her psychology, and so long as she continues faithful to herself and is not turned aside from her course by the opinions of others, it is likely to remain without any considerable change.

Like every educational method created by one mind with little regard for tradition, Montessori's system reflects the limitations of its author's personality. These limitations, if we may judge from her writings, are very great. Except for a religious

---

[1] Board of Education pamphlet, p. 23.

zeal which consorts badly with a materialistic conception of the human mind, her thought seems to be closely confined to its medical and scientific concerns. [There are no signs of appreciation of art in any form, and only a very partial indication of literary interest. Even her undoubted love of children, which is the driving power of her educational endeavour, has an element of hardness and austerity in it. The joyous play of the child makes no appeal to her. His toys are 'foolish and degrading'; his games are 'meaningless' and 'void of thought'; the stories commonly told to him are 'silly.' Montessori's ideal child never plays —except at *her* games; and then he is eager for knowledge, " a true son of that humanity which has been throughout centuries the creator of scientific and civil progress." [1] Continue his education on the lines begun in the Children's House, add religious instruction (perhaps inconsequently, but at Montessori's express desire), and there will appear in the end such another person as Montessori herself—one devoted to science, with a dash of religion, but with only a meagre æsthetic interest.]

But though Montessori's educational ideal expresses her personal limitations, it must not be thought that its defects are in any way peculiar or uncommon. They appear in some form in every plan of education, from Locke onward, in which

[1] *The Montessori Method*, p. 372.

education is regarded as confined in its origins to sensory experience. The sensationalist conception of mind as a synthesis of sensory elements exaggerates the passivity of the child in relation to his environment by representing learning as a process of receiving impressions. It puts under suspicion the active response of intellect or emotion as introducing a disturbing factor into mental process, and it tends to ignore the constructive expression of ideas as a mere by-product of receptivity. In this way, as we see very plainly in Montessori's scheme, every form of activity which is real self-activity in the sense of being brought about by an inner impulse rather than by a sensory stimulus is considered of little account in mental development. This applies to all kinds of childish art, to the emotional stirrings that prompt to song and dance as well as to the embodiment of thought in line or clay by means of drawing or modelling. Especially it applies to those arts that call imagination freely into play, whether passively in the appreciation of stories or actively in the dramatization of them. For the personal activities of imagination, in the view of Montessori as of all sensationalists, are not merely useless, but dangerous. They introduce an element of caprice into the orderly array of sense impressions and tamper with the truth of things that is supposed to be guaranteed by well-regulated senses. "Montessori does not encourage imagination," remarks one of her expositors, " because she feels that the strength of imagination is so great that it will fulfil its own work, and her business as an educator is to eliminate those thousands of false impressions which children get from being too fanciful." [1] The arts, and especially literature, of which fancy is the very soul, can only be allowed to enter the Montessori school on sufferance, if admitted at all. Nothing must be allowed to interfere with the prosaic instruction of the children " concerning the objects that constitute their daily environment." It is ' facts,' not ' fancies,' that Montessori would give them.

Another reason for the narrowness of Montessori's curriculum, also connected with the sensationalist conception of mental genesis, is her view of education as primarily a process of individual evolution. The effect of such a view, if it is not qualified by interpreting the first stages of life in the light of the last, is to throw a disproportionate emphasis on the child as a child. The obvious impulses and tendencies of the early years are treated as of most significance for the educator, and the crude beginnings of the higher life of the spirit, which are neither so strong nor so definite as the lower animal attributes, are generally overlooked or undervalued. The result is just such a restriction of the educational

[1] Miss Tozier's article on *The Montessori Apparatus*, in *The World's Work*, March 1912, p. 395.

programme to what may be called the natural aspects of human experience as appears in the Montessori system.

Now it is undoubtedly true that the child is but little developed in all that is most distinctively human, and that, apart from direct and even deliberate instruction from the mature adult, he is incapable of manifesting his human affinities. Follow Montessori's method even more strictly than Montessori and leave him to make his own discoveries in the spiritual world that is opened up to his elders by art and literature and religion, and the result will be an almost complete blankness of soul. But this does not warrant the limitation of education to subjects which lie well within the range of a child's experience. It may be a reason for caution lest we impose adult interests on him prematurely and in such fashion as to do violence to his proper development. It is not a reason for forgetting that one day he will be a man with none of these things alien to him, and that therefore he is more than he appears to be as a child and needs to be educated accordingly. The very fact that he grows into a being capable of appreciating a super-sensuous experience is clear proof that this capacity is present in rudiment from the beginning, even if in forms that are not readily discernible. It is what he becomes as well as what he is that gives us the key to the understanding of his nature, and we do him a grave injustice when we ignore his potentialities in estimating his present capacity. "We do not know the meaning either of his tendencies or of his performances excepting as we take them as germinating seed, or opening bud, of some fruit to be borne. The whole world of visual nature is all too small an answer to the problem of the meaning of the child's instinct for light and form. The entire science of physics is none too much to interpret adequately to us what is involved in some simple demand of the child for the explanation of some casual change that has attracted his attention. The art of Raphael or of Corot is none too much to enable us to value the impulses stirring in the child when he draws and daubs." [1]

Though all this has been said in criticism of Montessori's system, it is probable that she would not dissent from the general principle that underlies the argument. If her doctrine of the twofold manifestation of the life impulse in the body growth and the soul development of man does not quite imply the nascence of the æsthetic and kindred interests in early childhood, it is at any rate not inconsistent with the idea of their nascence then. It clearly indicates the existence of spontaneous activities of soul, among which we may be permitted to include those potentialities if we wish. Montessori, however, does not go so far herself. She has no

[1] Professor Dewey, *The School and the Child*, p. 30.

From Locke to Montessori

objection to children dancing or drawing, if they do so on their own initiative, but she does not consider performances of this kind as of educational value. She simply tolerates them because on her own principles she cannot refuse to allow any impulse that is not positively harmful to find expression for itself. The psychic activities of childhood which in her view are of consequence for education are the instinctive desire for knowledge that is behind the sensory education, and the religious sentiment. For the former there is of course ample provision in her system. The latter, she confesses, remains a problem for her pedagogy, but a problem she means to solve. The omission of religious education from her scheme, indeed, gives her as much concern as the absence of the humanities gives her critics; and she states the case for its establishment on grounds almost identical with theirs. " If religion is born with civilization, its roots must lie deep in human nature. We have had most beautiful proof of an instinctive love of knowledge in the child. Now in his liberty the child should show us, as well, whether man is by nature a religious creature." [1]

But Montessori's recognition of her own defects does not free her from the criticism directed against the omissions of her scheme. It rather confirms it by the partial admission of its truth in the case of religion. Here is a subject which on her own view

[1] *The Montessori Method*, p. 372.

Omission of the Humanistic Subjects

is of supreme importance and which yet has no place in her school. For what reason ? Presumably because it is difficult to reconcile any kind of instruction in a subject necessarily dogmatic with the fundamental principle of her method that all learning must be free and unforced. If, in spite of this, the fact that there is a religious sentiment which calls for satisfaction in childhood is made a plea for the introduction of a special education in the concerns of religion, it is certainly not possible to draw the line where Montessori tries to draw it. Precisely the same case which she makes out for religious education can be made out for any of the other subjects of a humanistic type which are not included in her educational scheme. The child, when left to himself, fails to reveal his æsthetic and cultural capacities in the same way as he fails to reveal his religious capacities. His unaided drawing, his untrained taste in song and story and dancing, are primitive in the extreme, but assuredly no more so than his native religion. But it does not follow from this, as one might infer from Montessori's practice, that religion and the arts have no proper place in an educational system in which the pupils are allowed liberty for development, and can only be introduced by some special device that effects a temporary reconciliation of freedom and dogma. The great delight which children show in drawing, singing, and literature, when their occupations have been appropriately chosen and introduced by the teacher, clearly demonstrates the kinship that exists between the child's soul and the beauty embodied in the works of adult culture and art. It is plain that the dogmatism necessary in this kind of instruction, though contrary to the principle of self-education as Montessori usually conceives it, is not an external imposition that does harm to the growth of mind and character, but is a means of setting free hidden powers which, when developed and exercised, give a new significance to childhood.

CHAPTER XIII

THE CHILDREN'S HOUSE

THE connexion of the Montessori system with the Children's Houses in which it made its first appearance was quite accidental. Signor Talamo, with a scheme for housing reform, wished special provision to be made for the care of the little children in his tenements and planned to set aside a house for their use. Dr Montessori gladly availed herself of the opportunity thus afforded to give practical effect to her own scheme of educational reform, and undertook to give them not merely care, but training. But with the development of Montessori's methods out of the experimental stage and the spread of her schools over the world the Children's Houses have almost entirely lost their original character as integral parts of the blocks of buildings in which the children live, and are now only houses for children in the general sense of being carefully adapted to the needs of little ones. In spite of this, the notion of a special place for the upbringing of children before the school age, better than the ordinary home and yet in most intimate contact with it, may still be considered a permanent feature of Montessori's educational ideal.

From Locke to Montessori

In an inaugural address delivered on the occasion of the opening of one of the first Children's Houses Montessori has indicated the significance, both for education and for social life, of this attempt to combine home and school.[1]

In the first place, she points out, it introduces a new idea in education by putting *the school within the home*. She agrees with all the educational reformers who regard the home as the central institution for the upbringing of the young. But she is too well aware of the state of matters in most homes under the conditions of modern life to think that ordinary parents can ever take any very considerable share in the education of their children. Instead of regretting the imperfections of things as they are, she accepts the situation and faces its problems. If the home cannot educate properly, then the school must make good its deficiencies: not the ordinary school, however, with its coercions and restraints and its remoteness from the common concerns of life, but a veritable Children's House, a school within the home, with all the freedom of the home and the skilled direction that is lacking in most homes. In this school within the home the parents will not educate their children themselves, but they will be in constant touch with all that goes on. They may come in at any hour of the day to watch the proceedings, and so learn to

[1] *The Montessori Method*, ch. iii.

take an interest in the training of their children which will lead them to co-operate with the teacher. Once this relation is established between teacher and parent the school will exert its influence on the parents as much as on the children, and bring about the modification in the whole social environment of the new generation without which no considerable reform of present evils can be expected.

In the second place, she goes on to say, it represents a beginning in *the communizing of the maternal functions*. The modern world is familiar with the advantages of the communistic transformation of the general environment that is illustrated by the collective use of railway carriages, street lights, telephones, etc., and by the enormous production of all kinds of useful articles by industrial co-operation. In the Children's Houses the same principle of combination for the satisfaction of common needs is extended to personal services. Social evolution has brought about great changes in home life. Woman has been forced by new social and economic conditions to give her time and strength to remunerative work outside the home, and it is no longer possible for her to do justice to her family duties. The only way of escape from the difficulties of the situation is to socialize the home by communizing the work of the servant, the nurse, the teacher. This is what has been done in the Children's Houses with regard to the care of the children. " We have in the Children's Houses a demonstration of this ideal which is unique in Italy or elsewhere. Its significance is most profound, for it corresponds to a need of the time. We can no longer say that the convenience of leaving her children takes away from the mother a natural social duty of first importance—namely, that of caring for and educating her tender offspring. No, for to-day the social and economic evolution calls the working woman to take her place among wage-earners, and takes away from her by force those duties which would be most dear to her! The mother must, in any event, leave her child. . . . We are, then, communizing a ' maternal function,' a feminine duty, within the house." If the idea thus realized is developed further it will in course of time bring about a complete reorganization of the home. Among other things, there might be a house-infirmary where the sick could be tended without losing touch with the family life, and a communal kitchen where the food of a whole group of families could be prepared. Such a transformation of domestic conditions would not destroy the home, as some people fear. On the contrary, it would give it a new and higher character by making the woman, like the man, " an individual, a free human being, a social worker."

There is room for difference of opinion concerning the desirability of the far-reaching social changes which Montessori sees foreshadowed in the Children's Houses. But quite apart from the question of the intrinsic value of the scheme she favours, her views on the social bearings of early education are entitled to the most serious consideration, as the mature opinions of a large-hearted, experienced woman on a matter which is of peculiar interest to women. Under any conditions, the upbringing of children in the first years of life is much more the concern of women than of men, not merely because most of the labour it involves is theirs, but even more because of the effects it has on the economy of the home and the social position of women. It is all to the good that we should have the important problems it raises discussed broadly and sanely from the feminine point of view.

The situation is certainly not a simple one either on the social or on the pedagogical side. Let us take the social question first. If the main argument for withdrawing children from their own homes and putting them under the expert care of nurses and teachers in any kind of institution external to the individual home is that mothers under the present industrial system are unable to find time to look after them themselves, the experiment rests on very insecure grounds. It is doubtful, to say the least, whether the encouragement which such a scheme gives to the employment of the house-mother in directly productive occupations is good for family life in any respect. It is certainly better for the half-deserted child that there should be a Children's House with open doors and that he should not be left entirely to his own devices in the absence of his mother at work; but the removal of the immediate evil does nothing to put an end to the disorganization of family life which is its cause. The chances are that it only serves to perpetuate it. The arrangement it presupposes is certainly unsound from the economic point of view. The additional earnings of the working woman are almost sure to be counterbalanced by the decreased wages of the class of men whose wives go out to work; and against such increase in joint income as there happens to be must be set the greater cost of managing the neglected home. Professional women and those in the higher grades of labour may contrive to gain their economic independence by means of non-domestic work, and escape in some measure the operations of the iron law of wages. There is no such escape for the women of the artisan class for whose benefit the Children's Houses were in the first instance established. These women have to look after their houses in some fashion after the day's work in shop or factory, with very inadequate financial compensation for the addition to their toil. An institution like the Children's Houses which makes it easier for the industrial exploitation of women to continue is assuredly not an unmixed blessing.

The Children's House

We do not do justice to the Children's House, however, if we think of it simply as a superior kind of crèche where children are cared for when their mothers go out to work. The working mother is only a special case, made unduly prominent, perhaps, by the conditions under which the Montessori system first took practical shape. On the broader view of social needs taken by Montessori the Children's House is meant to be a general convenience for all sorts and conditions of women. In these days many women who are not compelled to work to make ends meet are eager to extend their interests beyond the confines of the household, and would gladly do so if their lives were not used up in the incessant labour of attending to a house and a family. To them the communal performance of domestic tasks, exemplified by the Children's House, offers a way of escape from bondage. With the preparation of food in common kitchens and the education of children in a little school in touch with the home, as Montessori suggests, there is no reason why mothers should not employ the leisure gained by deputing part of their responsibilities for the broadening of their own lives. Such a plan might very well be of advantage to themselves and to all dependent on them. Put on the lowest terms, it may be regarded as a serviceable device (like the vacuum cleaner or the fireless cooker) for reducing routine work which in the aggregate is so burdensome as to make women little more than means to the well-being of others. Perhaps it even deserves to be described as a partial transfer to the community of duties which in their result are always of more than personal significance. However it be considered, it represents an aspiration after a fuller and freer life on the part of women with which every right-minded person must sympathize. The only question is whether the method proposed is the right one for the attainment of this most desirable object; and to that no general answer can be given. If the desire to be ' an individual' and to lead ' a free, human life,' on which Montessori rightly lays so much stress, involves such a complete surrender of the maternal functions to others that the controlling influence of the child's life is not the mother but the teacher, the help given by the Children's House or any institution of the kind simply defeats its own ends.[1] The proper function of the school at any age, and most of all in early childhood, is to give assistance to the home in doing the work which, with all its imperfections, it can do better than any other

[1] Though I see no reason why the Children's House as conceived by Montessori should not be a real help to a mother in the fulfilment of her maternal duties, I am inclined to think that her plans for the care of the children of the working classes are open to the serious objection that they take away from the mother all her spiritual obligation to her children, and leave her with only a servant's part to play. It may be good for the children to be in the Children's House from nine to five in the winter and eight to six in the summer (*The Montessori Method*, p. 120), but what about the mother?

The Children's House

social institution. The mother who allows another to usurp her place in the upbringing of her children does grievous wrong both to her children and to herself. The freedom she acquires by entrusting their souls to an alien care is purchased by the loss of her own soul. Life for every one, man and woman alike, gets its value, not from the goods that are possessed or produced, but from the human relationships that one creates for oneself; and for a woman in particular it is the natural ties of home life, maintained and enriched by personal service, which are the very core of individuality and a free existence. Life without other relationships may be poor: without these it is absolutely destitute.

The educational side of the question, to which we now turn, is closely connected with the social side. If, as Montessori asserts, there are many mothers who are either unwilling or unable to bring up their own children properly, there is obvious need for places of infant education like the Children's Houses which are more suitable for the little ones than the ordinary home. The modern school already supplements the home at so many points that no objection can be made on general principle to this extension of its functions to young children before the usual age of entering the public school. The medical inspection of scholars, indeed, has made evident the need for the systematic supervision of children from birth. If there is an educational need as well as a medical, there is no good reason for refusing the young child the teacher's care in the first years of life.

But the case for the Montessori system, as stated by its supporters, is stronger than this. The Children's House, in their view, is not merely one of a number of possible agencies for the education of certain children living under somewhat exceptional social conditions. To them it seems the best for all children, because it meets and satisfies a universal need of childhood which is not being adequately satisfied in any other way. Even in the best homes, they would maintain, there is not the necessary apparatus for the training of the senses, and opportunities are not or cannot be given for the independent, unrestricted activity which is essential for self-education. As for the existing infant schools (including the kindergartens), which might give the little pupils the education they require, the only thing to be said is that either they do not do it or only do it very imperfectly. Consequently the only institution really suitable for young children is the Children's House, or some establishment on similar lines.

In discussing the arguments put forward for the universal adoption of the Montessori methods, it is impossible to deny that there is some truth in the criticism of the home on which they are based. The ordinary home is certainly not an ideal place for the nurture of infancy. Houses are constructed for

The Children's House

adults, and many of the petty misdemeanours which disturb the even tenor of the child's moral development are due to that fact. Grown-up modes of behaviour and thought, as little suited to the infant mind as the usual furniture to the little body, cause other difficulties. Even the restriction of social relations and the concern about individual well-being, which make the family influence so effective in the determining of character, may engender lifelong morbidities of mind and temper.[1] But while these defects of the home may be taken to justify the beginnings of some form of education in special schools at an early age, they do not give any direct support to the case for the Children's House. After it has been agreed that children may possibly profit by an education better adapted to their needs than that generally received in the home, it remains to be settled whether that which Montessori advocates is the inevitable education for the purpose.

The view we take of that claim depends on whether we accept her contention that specific sense-training in early childhood is indispensable for the perfection of the later developments of mind. There are other elements in her system besides the sensory exercises. But if that part be rejected—

---

[1] Freud and the other psycho-analysts have demonstrated this in some very startling ways. See various articles by Freud, Jung, etc., in *The American Journal of Psychology*, 1909.

From Locke to Montessori

and we have seen that there is a strong case against it—most of what is distinctive in the system would go with it. What remains is certainly not of sufficient consequence to warrant the conclusion that all children should go as a matter of course to the Children's House at the age of three. Those parts of the sensory training which experience has proved to be of some value can easily be absorbed into other systems of infant education. The Montessori variety of freedom may only be possible in conjunction with the didactic apparatus, but all the freedom that is either desirable or possible at this stage of development is capable of being enjoyed by any child whose parent or teacher realizes the need for it: the Children's House has no monopoly of the spirit of freedom. As for writing and reading, which appear in the Montessori curriculum *faute de mieux*, there is no reason why they should not be postponed for three or four years till the children are in a position to make use of them.

Apart altogether from the question of the necessity for sense-training or any other specialized training in early childhood, the pretension of the Children's House or any form of school to the foremost place in the educational beginnings of every child is one which cannot be lightly admitted.

It still remains to be proved that even the best institution can be trusted to take the place of the ordinary home in the upbringing of the young. The

The Children's House

Children's Houses may be conducted for a time in the fine spirit of their founder and show such satisfactory results in child culture as to make good mothers raise the ' searching and painful question ' as to " whether the Casa dei Bambini will not ultimately be the Home for all our children." [1] But the record of many excellent endeavours of a similar kind furnishes only too much reason for misgivings about the future. Dr Montessori will not always be at hand to guide and inspire the movement. The exceptional women whose pioneer enthusiasm has given it its successful beginning will be followed by more commonplace people who have little of their high purpose and who pay more attention to the letter than to the spirit of the methods they direct. When that day comes, as it surely will, the discovery, old but ever new, will be made that the best place for the first education of children is not the Children's House, but the father and mother's house. The fact that in a great many cases the homes of the common people do not provide very satisfactory conditions for the little ones who grow up in them [2] may be a reason for the existence

---

[1] Mrs Fisher, *A Montessori Mother*, p. 141.

[2] Care should be taken not to exaggerate the undoubted evils. A poor home is not necessarily a bad home, as many middle-class people are apt to assume. Pestalozzi's ideas about early education, under the bad conditions which attended the beginnings of the factory system, are well worthy of attention at the present time. His robust faith in the possibilities of the ordinary mother may still inspire us to an optimistic view of the potential educational value of the poor home.

of the Children's Houses as a temporary expedient. It does not justify the claim that as substitutes for the home they are an institution of permanent social value. Dr Montessori derides the contrivance of a hygienic school bench on the ground that it assumes the continuance of an intolerable state of matters in the school. Her own scheme of Children's Houses is open to the same objection. If the homes in which the children live are not good enough for them, the cure is not to be found in the establishment of an institution which might conceivably help to perpetuate the economic evils which have spoiled family life and lowered its educational influence, but in the reorganization of society so as to secure better homes. The suggestion is not utopian. In all civilized countries to-day the housing problem and allied problems affecting the home are becoming increasingly urgent; and in some countries the first steps have already been taken toward the endowment of motherhood and the home in those cases where widowhood or some like cause would prevent the mother attending to the upbringing of her family. It is along these lines rather than by the establishment of Children's Houses that the difficulties created by the defects of modern home life are likely to be overcome.

INDEX

269

From Locke to Montessori

Index

271